Sobre
684-0254

INDIA

1 The eastern quadrant of the Samrat Yantra, Jaipur

INDIA
PEOPLE AND PLACES

RICHARD LANNOY

---

188 PHOTOGRAVURE PLATES

SIX IN COLOUR

INTRODUCTORY ESSAY

AND NOTES

THE VANGUARD PRESS · NEW YORK

For
all my Indian friends
in gratitude for their encouragement
and kindness

TEXT PRINTED IN GREAT BRITAIN BY JARROLD AND SONS LTD NORWICH 1955
GRAVURE PRINTED BY CLARKE AND SHERWELL LTD NORTHAMPTON

Shortly after arriving in India, while wandering in the back streets of Bombay, I was suddenly startled by crude vermilion stones representing the popular deities, Hanuman the monkey, and Ganesa the elephant-headed. Close by was a sacred pipal tree, round which generations of worshippers had wound threads of cotton, an ancient custom, so that the gnarled tree-trunk had acquired a strange fibrous tissue, daubed with blood-coloured dust. In Aurangabad, Deccan, I visited a dark temple under another sacred tree, and in a niche was a huge vermilion stone, polished to an almost aggressive shine, crudely shaped into a head with a snub nose and staring moronic eyes. At first I was shocked by a feeling of gross, malignant power in the image, until gradually I recognized in the almost indecent nakedness of the red stone, of the gnome-like features, a fantastic representation of Ganesa, carved not by any great artist but by one of the million anonymous craftsmen of the Indian villages.

It is such weird, often grotesque images, which receive a daily anointing with oil, or are frequently smeared with coloured powder, that prove so alarming to the foreigner. How, I wondered, could a religion which produced a world of lofty conceptions of the Divine also create these curious, sub-human deities, in whose inflamed vitality there was a suggestion of primeval power? Because of the great disparity that seems to exist between levels of culture in India, it took me some time to understand that primitive Hinduism is still in existence side by side with more subtle religious observances. It persists because there is a profound need among the villagers for religious imagery approximating to their own daily experience. The religious art of the great ancient epochs has come to an end in India, but throughout the country the making of images, almost alarmingly primitive in style, has continued on the same lines for centuries. These images, as well as the products of many other crafts connected with the Hindu seasonal festivals—toys, pottery, banners, and the murals on the houses—are a revelation of the richly imaginative lives of Indian people. Today they are an exciting proclamation of an undiminished vitality, nowhere better shown than in Indian village life.

*   *   *

The first experience I had of rural life was at Badami, which remains in my memory as the loveliest of all the villages I have seen. One travels down long avenues of big trees, through

5

rocky country of a rich earth-red colour, until the horseshoe crescent of orange rock at Badami rises abruptly from the plain. The houses, too, are built of the same coloured earth, their roofs moulded in simple contours. The shapes at Badami are all gentle, so that one might imagine the town to be a centre of pottery. But it is its ancient carving that has given this little place a beautiful sculptural quality. On the crests of rock are some very early constructed temples, their rounded towers subtly echoing the curious stratified formations of the cliffs. Carved into the face of the rock is a group of four of the finest of Indian cave temples, dating from the sixth century, which display an acute sensibility to both the natural rock forms and the setting of brightly coloured flowering trees. Age has further enhanced the beauty of the stone constructions which one sees everywhere, for the carvings, and in particular the stone steps of the village tank, have acquired a battered surface which contributes to the shaping of all forms into a well-worn, harmonious whole. Thus age has split and crumbled the cliffs and boulders and caused the flight of steps to subside gently, fissures to open between the slabs, and creepers to thrust through the stone temple towers. Instead of causing Badami to present a forlorn appearance, time has miraculously drawn the village closer into harmony with the parent rocks, at the foot of which it rests like a beast in front of its cave.

In the streets the women, wearing the deep wine-coloured, emerald-bordered saris of the region and carrying on their heads brass vessels of water from the village well, wind their way among earth-crusted houses and across patterns of sunlight spilt by yellow-leaved trees. Beside gnarled roots are collected some of the old carvings from long-vanished shrines, figures of Ganesa, the elephant god, and slabs bearing the crested hoods of the Naga serpent god. Monkeys imitate their stone counterpart, Hanuman, and cattle, their horns painted red and green with brass finials on the points, nose among scraps. Women sit sorting grain, the hiss of seeds on wicker being the only sound besides that of stone cutters chipping at millstones on the roadsides, one of the principal industries of the village. Children play under the wheels of a processional chariot which has wooden panels carved with cavorting figures of demons. Men sit on bullock carts piled high with sacks of grain, their heads swathed in cerise or lemon-yellow turbans. In the dry, sunbaked field near by, where figures are crouched over the crops, one catches an intimation of the monotony and harsh reality of bare necessity; but underlying it there is a feeling of quiet acceptance, and frequently one receives the broad flash of a smile, betraying a thread of happiness in spite of the daily toil.

In the late afternoon sun, when it is cooler, the women go out to look at the stocks of saris in the village store, or watch the goldsmith at work on bracelets they have ordered for the occasion of a family wedding, while others climb the steps leading to the cave temples, to offer flowers and butter to the gods. In the caves are dramatic scenes of Vishnu in his incarnations as lion and boar; on the ceilings celestial figures drift in a cloud, the serpent king spirals forth from clustered foliage, and in the dark recesses there are tender scenes of love. More than thirteen hundred years old, these magnificent sculptures were very possibly carved by ancestors of the present inhabitants; but it is not archaeological interest, nor aesthetic awareness, that brings the villagers to them today. These caves are their house of God, in which are stored the intimate longings and aspirations of the community. Although few places in India can boast

6

11 Durbar of H. H. the late Maharana of Udaipur

such exquisite works of art, every village has its shrine, and however poor the people may be these are always large enough to leave the imagination space to roam.

*

South of Badami the country becomes, in summer, harsh and arid, without the softening effect of green crops, particularly that greenest of greens, a rice-field. At this time of year the high, thickly ornamented temple towers for which South India is renowned stand out even more emphatically against the flat yellow expanse of the plains, dominating, and by the force of their size almost overpowering the lives of the people, whose ancestors went to such fantastic lengths in the scorching heat to erect a symbol of their faith. The temple cities of the south in many ways resemble the medieval cities of Europe. Life revolves round the central focal-point of the community, a great temple, and the feelings of the people are focused upon the various seasonal festivals, when gold and silver processional images are paraded through the streets. The power of the temples is on the decline, but many people are still employed by them; revenue is collected from the temple lands, and rice and coconut plantations are cultivated to supply food for the offerings given daily in the shrines of the deities.

From a distance the formal simplicity of the towers surrounded by a succession of walls can be truly impressive. But inside, the lavish ornamentation and profusion of carved figures are often bewildering for the visitor. The temples are best seen at night, when the colonnades, ghostly and deserted by day, are caverns containing a thousand flickering lamps, the sculpture banked in groves and forests on all sides, awesome in the curious, fierce glow of the flames. To enhance this fantasy still further, the musicians play upon drums and a harsh-sounding hautboy, to the accompaniment of many gongs and the ancient conch; it is a primeval sound that reaches a tremendous crescendo at the climax of the ceremony, when the priest brings to the image deep at the end of a long corridor in the innermost sanctuary, a candelabrum studded with many camphor lamps. In some temples this ceremony of lights, during which the images of the deities are worshipped, is performed at more than one shrine; at Suchindram, where I witnessed a particularly impressive evening "Puja", the last shrine contains no image, but instead, in the central niche, a single mirror in which the whole impressive scene is reflected.

*

Successive phases of Indian civilizations have left behind them cities mysteriously abandoned or ruthlessly plundered and of these probably the most romantic is the city of Vijayanagar. It is a gigantic ruin situated in a natural fortress of hills, across which are strewn boulders in chaotic disorder, resembling a crowd of elephants that have suddenly become petrified. Vijayanagar was the last great empire of South India; it wielded enormous power over the peninsula and acquired fabulous wealth, which it lavished on the building of triumphal pavilions, palaces and temples. Founded as a Hindu bastion against the oncoming Muslim invaders from the north in the fourteenth century, it ruled the south for two centuries, until it was sacked after the battle of Talikota in 1565. Now a ruin partly covered in thickets of cactus and thorn, the huge stone constructions still suggest the fierce splendour of a great martial power. But the magnitude of these ruins is not overpowering, for the surfaces of the

7

great stones are covered with delightful scenes in relief depicting royal processions, horses, elephants, and dancing girls leaping with joyous abandon. The sculptor was obviously undaunted by the sheer size and seriousness of the subject, for we find, among the lizards scurrying across the hot stone, imitations of these creatures carved on the ledges with life-like realism.

With considerable engineering skill the people of Vijayanagar constructed an irrigation system, which brought life-giving water from the Tungabhadra river to their arid stronghold, for fields of rice and cool pleasure gardens. This system has in part survived the devastation which overtook the city at the battle of Talikota, and it affords an interesting comparison with another gigantic, but modern, construction, the Tungabhadra dam, a few miles away from the ruins.

*

One thing generally overlooked when one is surrounded by the exuberance of detail in India, is that a deeper sense of order underlies the richness of surface. The Indian tower, in all its variety of forms, is an object of stern geometrical beauty. The walls of most buildings dedicated to Siva (and in South India the temples are more usually Saivite) are ornamented with bold stripes in red and white, which increase the formal effect, while the arrangement of towers and courtyards conforms to a rigid pattern laid down in sacred texts. These plans, known as Yantras, are similar to the diagrams, mandalas and geometrical patterns used for direction and concentration during meditation. The feeling for the geometrical takes many forms in South India, but it is revealed at its best at the very southernmost point of the peninsula, at Cape Comorin, where it assumes monumental simplicity. Set above the rocks, against which the waves of the southern ocean beat, is a broad terrace, surmounted by a high wall striped red and white, and enclosing the temple of Kanya Kumari. With the minimum of formal simplicity a great country faces the ocean; a solemn, dazzling wall, over the top of which can be seen the polished finial of the temple tower.

Farther round the coast at Mamallapuram, near Madras, a group of temples again illustrates this point. Close to the shore, in temple, shrine and boulder reliefs, the sculptors carved what are perhaps some of the friendliest, most charming sculptures in India. Suffused with a gentle feeling for nature akin to that found in the Ajanta frescoes, they are yet remarkably austere in structure: but the rough surface of the stone, the crisp stratified ledges of the pavilion towers, are relieved from harshness by the soft, rounded forms of elephants in relief, lovers clinging to the shadows of their niches, angels flying across the crest of a curving boulder, wild animals suckling their young. Mamallapuram reminds us that to India the world owes many of its famous animal fables, and that early collections such as the *Panchatantra*, the *Jatakas*, and the *Hitopadesa*, which found their way into medieval European tradition by way of Persia, provided material for writers from Boccaccio and Chaucer to La Fontaine.

*

The west coast, the fabled shore of Malabar, with its spices that for a long time were a lure to Arabs and to the European merchant adventurer, is very different from the rest of South India, having customs of its own and a luxuriant tropical vegetation watered by the monsoon when it strikes the western ghats. Here, in Travancore, we find a network of water ways and rice-fields enclosed between swathes of thickly planted palm groves. In most parts of India sun and dust are the elements with which man must wrestle, but in Travancore it is water that conditions existence. People have surrendered to it rather than built an elaborate defence against it: one may see a line of women hurrying along a narrow pathway from taking a bath, their saris wet and still clinging to their bodies, like a procession of water nymphs. The canals run into narrow creeks, black or green tunnels of mud and palm roots, as if all were turning to coal. Huts and stores are dilapidated, decaying parts sagging beneath crisp new carpentry; and the jetties on to the main waterways are nodes around which life revolves and erodes. The back and forth of boats, the up and down of water, the slow arc of the sun, the swift crescent of the monsoon storm are the momentum of river life.

Everything is made by hand, requiring inventiveness or traditional skill: shelter from sun and rain is created with an armoured thatch of palm fronds, and steering beneath this thatch like a weaver's shuttle is the sleek form of the long pointed boat. Architecture as such can scarcely exist, owing to the inevitable impermanence of shelter. Coolie hats and leaf umbrellas bob up and down in the rice-fields, making men look like horned insects in a swamp.

The popular art-form of Malabar is the Kathakali dance drama; its strange, exotic move-ments, verging on a formalized representation of ferocity, are strikingly similar to the movements of dances of other tropical palm regions of the Far East. In the old palace at Mattancheri is a series of fine sixteenth-century frescoes depicting scenes from the *Ramayana*. They are some of the most dramatic paintings in India, with rich, deep colours, the figures parading as proud as peacocks, in splendid warlike array, with glistening feathers and head-dresses of flowers. More than any photograph could do, these frescoes evoke the wild, dramatic scenes of Kathakali dancing which, during local festivals, lasts throughout the night.

*   *   *

Of supreme importance as we pass from South to North India are the caves of Ajanta and Ellura. Formerly situated in kingdoms which overlapped into both regions, and bearing the marks of both northern and southern cultural influences, they illustrate to a marked degree the splendour and subtlety of ancient and medieval India. Many elements go to make up one's experience—the frescoes and the sculpture, the gorges and ravines, the turbulence of the monsoon sky, the peasants working among the tall maize stalks—each a fragment of great beauty and a part of the magnificent whole. Indeed, the caves themselves are in a fragmentary state that enhances rather than detracts from the essential mystery one feels on personally discovering the vestiges of a great past in these sequestered monasteries and temples. The smashed rock carvings, the raw stone revealed between the scarred paintings are like the darkness of dreams, while the strange, withdrawn expressions of the languorous princesses, the smooth elliptical smile of the stone-eyed gods suggest divine and celestial creatures for ever fixed in the sublime peace of immortality. After the insistent glare of the southern sun, the soft greens of Ajanta and the sound of a waterfall spilling into the great horseshoe ravine give one the feeling of being in the presence of a more kindly nature than that which invests the intensely arid and flat plains of South India. The caves are hollowed from a sheer rock precipice around which deep grass and broad-leaved trees form a dense carpet, where the gold-and-red tongues of the exquisite *Gloriosa superba* lily clamber over the trees, and water rushes echoing through a chaos of tumbled boulders. Here, in isolation, one feels the secrecy and remoteness of the Buddhist caves, carved between the first century B.C. and the sixth century A.D.; for many centuries they were lost beneath thick jungle creepers, to be rediscovered by chance little more than a hundred years ago.

It is a delight to find that the brightly coloured scenes depicted in the Ajanta frescoes are suffused with gentle feeling for animals and flowers, while the supple linear contours of the figures are a perfect medium for portraying a luxurious ease of movement. It is paradoxical that Buddhism, with its central theme of renunciation, of the extinction of desire, should have produced some of the most exquisite of all Asia's figure paintings, for what finally remains uppermost in one's memory are the graceful, lambent-eyed princesses, their soft, round flesh subtly moulded and tinted. In the drawing of curled finger-tips, spiralled locks of hair, and pearl necklaces that rise and dip over their swaying figures, as well as the tenderness with which the artists rendered gesture and touch, there is a highly cultivated sensuousness. But in counter-poise between the ample curvature of their bodies and the indrawn gaze of their eyes can be sensed that moment between giving and final renunciation; for in such scenes as the beautiful "Dying Princess" there is an infinite sadness, and the slanting eyes of the women appear to withdraw from us into stillness. In the sculpture, the round and curvilinear character of the forms is never broken but remains an even flow in and out of the matrix, while shallow encrustations of foliage clinging to the ornamented borders and pillars enhance this effect.

Whereas at Ajanta it is the paintings with their rich colour that are most important, at Ellura, a gigantic enterprise in rock carving, there remain far fewer paintings and it is the grave solemnity of the rock that is so deeply impressive. The individual carvings at Ellura are not so memorable as many elsewhere in India, but it is in the very magnitude of the almost abstract carving of shrines and temples that the unrivalled grandeur of the site lies. The sculptors seem to have been held in thrall by the solemn grey-brown stone, and sought to render the sheer might of rock precipices and caverns. The masterpiece of Ellura is the temple of Kailasanath, a vision conceived in rock of Mount Kailasa, the colossal legendary abode of the gods, far away to the north in the eternal snows of the Himalayas. One might think that the scale of this project would have been enough to daunt the sculptors, for it was hewn solid from the living rock and pierced with colonnades and spacious shrines with the sole aid of the small Indian chisel. Many sculptors over a period of some two hundred years contributed to the carving of this temple, and thanks to them the pilgrim to Ellura can still, a thousand years later, participate in the great dream of the Indian race; to aspire to those sublime heights and to glimpse in the carved mountain peaks the Indian vision of immortality. At the base of the temple, where light seldom penetrates, can be seen terrifying scenes of battle between gods and Titans, demons and fabulous beasts, which appear to support on their backs the entire, massive structure. Above, rise tier on tier of the towers, and across the high walls the sun catches the swirling draperies of flying celestial figures, while still higher appear the pinnacles of Kailasa, serenely austere, where sits Lord Siva enthroned among the angelic orders. There is no noise, except that of wind upon stone, the sound of *silence* itself.

*

Ajanta and Ellura belong to a gentle, fertile region, protected from invasion in the north by the Vindhya mountains and the Narbada river, but their art does not deny the vital energy which has impelled Indians to perform monumental feats of creation, without departing from their tolerant religious humanism. These temples, and the flowering of the arts associated with the Gupta period and other dynasties, represent one of the peaks of ancient cultural achieve-ment; but their completion marks the point of transition to the grave disturbances that befell India during her medieval period. The prolonged wars of this ensuing period shifted the emphasis from humanist art more emphatically towards religion, closely allied to martial prowess and feudalism. The area in which this drama was mainly enacted was to the north in Rajputana, or the modern State of Rajasthan, and the Punjab.

During the Muslim invasions from the north-west, which embroiled India in periodic wars from the early eleventh century until the establishment of the Moghul Empire five hundred years later, the most effective defence became concentrated round the escarpments and mountain retreats of Rajputana—a romantic region, with gigantic fortified palaces and walled cities, where the blue-blooded dynasties of militant Hindu India withstood repeated invasion.

The white marble city of Udaipur, lying beside a lake and surrounded by hills, is one of the most perfect of man-made scenes in India; encircled by a wall, white and shining in the sun, with its enormous palace and marble pavilions, it is the loveliest embodiment of feudal pride and regal power. Rajputana is a dry region, which for centuries lacked sufficient resources of its own to keep it at peace for long; as a result its occupants were driven to make frequent raids upon the cultivators of neighbouring fertile valleys. The cities still show an instinctive feeling for gathering up into strongholds the dispersed riches of more arid surrounding regions. Thus one finds more than anywhere else in India a pervading tendency to concentrate brilliant colour within limited space: courtyards, walled gardens, enamelled inlay, jewelled costumes, a school of miniature painting, secluded pavilions embellished with crowded murals; and, as if anxious to draw into the tiniest space the vast panorama of palace and mountain, multi-faceted mirror inlay, reflecting a thousandfold the image of the surrounding marble splendour. The style itself is derived from the Persian, and craftsmen from the Middle East left a profound impress upon the region. Rajput culture, however, radically differs from both Persian and Moghul art in its love of geometrical areas of intense colour, and originally its school of painting evolved from the style of ancient murals. The refinement of Moghul and Persian art, its love of minute detail and decorative arabesque undoubtedly contributed much to Rajput art, yet the Hindu culture transformed these elements into a more uncompromising power of mood and emotion to suit its own temperament.

Repeated conflict has left ancient North India ruined, and it is the medieval epoch that is most apparent, particularly in Rajputana. The philosophical subtleties of ancient India underwent a considerable transformation in the ninth century under the influence of Sankara and in the eleventh under that of Ramanuja. The complexities of Hindu religion became more elaborate, and at the same time were "driven underground", in the sense that the schools of mysticism withdrew into solitude, away from the Muslim proselytism, while Bhakti, meaning approximately love and devotion, formulated in the new vernacular languages, became the popular trend among a people who suddenly were faced with alarming threats to their contem-plative calm from the north-west. By his prowess in war the heroic figure of Rama became an increasingly popular deity to inspire devotion, as the Aryan lived once again the epic struggles of righteous warfare. At the same time as the theme of militant devotion swept across India there arose also a compensatory gentleness, in the cult of Krishna and Radha, expressive of the anguish of separation, the ecstasy of union, the raising of the erotic on to the transcendental plane—possibly an identification of the warrior's own predicament and that of the devoted wife separated from her husband during the long years of war, with that of the story of Krishna's divine love for Radha. Nowhere more richly than in Rajputana and the Punjab hills did this religious feeling inspire and suffuse the painting of the period. The wife pining for her husband within the confines of the palace, the feeling of pent-up longing, suggested by dark, stormy skies; or the return of the warrior amidst the excited flurries of the womenfolk, their saris a gaudy pattern of excitement—these are the favourite subjects of Rajput and Punjab Hill painting. At the termination of the campaigning seasons there would be festivals with dancing and music, and in the long months of enforced idleness a style of court art flourished that was inseparably linked with the mood of the season, the different times of day, the dramas of passion, embodied within the cult of Radha and Krishna.

A Rajput festival is at once a painting come alive and an interpretation of the ferociously brilliant colours we can find in mural and miniature. The school still survives in part today, for large murals, annually renewed on the walls of palace, temple, and house, are popular; and although these do not show the skill and subtlety of painting in the grand manner, they are nevertheless fresh and alive.

Rajput streets are some of the most lively in India; laughing, jolly families seated round the show-cases of the jewellers, looking at enormous silver bangles; children flying kites made of brightly coloured patterns that remind one of paintings by Paul Klee; the pavements round the dyers' shops running with lemon and crimson, while the dyers walk back and forth with wet cloth billowing out in the breeze as it dries; vendors arranging clay tops on the pavement; potters carrying on their heads huge panniers containing many large clay water-vessels; the street photographers hanging out their painted backcloths; avenues of dark stalls ablaze with deep red and green cotton prints or embroidered slippers and dazzling pigtails; painters at work on scenes for the backs of the rickshaws; groups of women hurrying by in crimson wedding saris embroidered with silver flowers. Some of them belong to the Jain religion with its great respect for all animal life; which is why the women can be seen sprinkling sugar for the ants on their way to worship at the temple.

Of the many mural paintings that once existed in old Rajput palaces scarcely any remain today; among those that have been preserved, the loveliest are in the palace of Bundi. This walled city has a beautiful lake with island temples in its mirror-smooth water, and above rises a steep rock escarpment on which stands the colossal fortified palace, romantic and apparently unassailable. The entrance leads up steep flights of steps through large gateways decorated with life-size blue elephants. The rooms are connected by a honeycomb of narrow corridors and dark stairways. Behind these walls the traveller can discover for himself a world of fantasy, a fable from a picture-book of legends, where he can people his imagination with the ghosts of jewelled princesses and turbaned princes. It is impossible to imagine a more idyllic setting for a tiny courtyard filled with flowers, the colonnades covered with frescoes. These were executed during the eighteenth century and are coloured emerald and turquoise, aquamarine and peacock blue, a characteristic colour key of Islamic art in Persia, whence this work derives part of its character. Besides this exquisite colouring, the scenes, mostly from the legends of Krishna, have a tender lyricism that casts a spell over the lone visitor in the hushed silence of the deserted courtyard. There is a great battle piece from the *Mahabharata*, and scenes of ladies sporting on swings during the spring festival of Holi, among marble pavilions and pleasure gardens with ornamental fish pools, jade birds in enamelled foliage, camels under the broad-leaved plantains. This is one of the most beautiful scenes in India and a veritable garden of paradise, an emerald fairy-tale.

*

In their festivals, music and crafts the villagers have expressed their hopes and fears, celebrated victory and prosperity, lamented the misery of defeat, poverty, and foreign occupation. In recent years the tragic upheaval of Partition has left a deep scar on two regions, the Punjab and Bengal, while mass-production and unemployment have accelerated a crisis in village life. Nevertheless, what I saw in many villages, particularly in Bengal, gave me an impression that the crafts stand a very good chance of survival. This cannot be proved statistically or even in argument; it can only be felt after visiting many villages. Immense sums of money have been allocated for the betterment of rural life, with emphasis on the specific demands and traditions of the village; it is a matter of government policy not to impose the ways of the town on villagers, for India is deeply mistrustful of a western-styled industrial revolution. But in Bengal, famous for its culture and a province more independent-minded perhaps than any other region, I was struck by the innate vitality of people as yet untouched by any government schemes, while having been most hard hit by Partition.

About six miles within India from the East Pakistan border (Bengal is partitioned into two States, one forming East Pakistan, while West Bengal remains in the Indian union), there is a village once owned by Muslims. At the time of Partition these men went to Pakistan and exchanged land there with Hindus coming into India. For five years the new Hindu occupants of the village were almost destitute. They completely reorganized the cultivation of land, and for years struggled on a minimum subsistence level, until they had recently their first successful rice crop with the aid of a tractor bought by one of the landlords and loaned to the other cultivators. With their new-found prosperity they built neat new thatched houses, using beautiful traditional designs of the region, and made their villages spotlessly clean. Originally craftsmen rather than farmers, their first instinctive celebration of success was to build round, wicker-woven grain stores, the plaited patterns picked out in colour, the door a panel of wood painted with symbolic decorations, the steps moulded to include a small niche in which to burn a light as a thank-offering to the goddess. Instead of old traditions being finally swept away in a flood of science and technology, there is a new activity arising from the age-old instinctive association of fertility with custom, crafts and seasonal rites.

*

There are still, in remote regions, tribes of aboriginals, who thousands of years ago retired into the forests and hills as a result of successive foreign invasions. These tribes are of indigenous pre-Dravidian stock; known as "Animists", they are not Hindus, although missionaries had some success in converting many to Christianity. Some of these aboriginals, like the Konds of Orissa, are extremely primitive, others, like the Santals, on the borders of Bengal and Bihar, more developed. Yet words like "primitive" and "undeveloped" are inadequate to describe people whose way of life is in many ways richer and more satisfactory than that of the more usual village communities of Hindu India.

It was spring when I arrived in the Santal region, and the villages glowed with filtered yellow sunlight from tall trees as yet fresh and free of the dust which obscures the brilliant greens in the long dry summer. The houses are made of mud, beautifully moulded into geometrical shapes, and enhanced with white, grey and red plaster, and it would be hard to find better kept villages anywhere. A dance had been arranged in the main village street, and the musicians gathered to announce the event by beating their drums. Women gradually assembled in crisp, bright garments: white saris with red borders and long silver necklaces. They carried freshly picked spring leaves hung upon cymbals, and forming into a line began to dance and sing. The Santals are handsome, dark-skinned people, their dances almost sternly simple. The drummers danced in a circle, weaving a complicated pattern in front of the women as well as a complex rhythm of sound, while the women advanced in small steps, inch by inch up an avenue of trees through which the evening sun pierced a sparkling pattern on the roadway and on the walls of houses, as if it were an integral part of the dance itself. Here was complete, indivisible composition, a perfect fusion of patterns in colour and sound, the ideal which in western ballet is striven for with the less subtle aid of artfully contrived light and stage technique. While the sun remained, the visual aspect was in itself sufficiently complex to demand the barest simplicity of movement; but as the light failed and the splashes of sun vanished, the dancers' movements became more agile, the music more emphatic in its rhythm. Green sap, yellow sun, the brilliance of white walls, the red earth, all were contained and animated in the dance of green leaves, silver jewellery, white robes, red borders, while the music of the drums seemed to be the *sound* of spring, earthen heaviness suddenly quickening with the new vernal fertility.

In Calcutta, West Bengal, I visited a folk music congress although at first I had been suspicious of its purpose and programme. But here were villagers who had never seen a stage before, had never known the meaning of stage-fright, performing, leaping about, singing, dancing with such unselfconscious abandon that they had to be forcibly removed from the stage when they threatened to hold up the show. Hindu and Muslim musicians were even invited from Pakistan, which is remarkable, since it was not so very long ago that Calcutta witnessed tragic scenes of bloodshed between the two religious communities. While outside during the interval, we were suddenly electrified by a song of quite extraordinary intensity and power. Hurrying back to our seats, we discovered that a group of musicians—an old man, his son, and a disciple—had begun their performance, the old man dressed in a multi-coloured robe of patches, the others in white cloaks, their hair swept into the traditional sleek cone of the extraordinary wandering sect of musicians known as Bauls. In spite of the wildly unconventional garb here, in this hymn to Krishna, was unmistakably true musical genius, which hushed the audience and held them in a spell of enchantment for nearly two hours. The old man, Nabani Das, is probably the finest living Baul musician, a great figure in the true folk tradition of the wandering minstrel.

At his home in Suri we sat under an awning in the midst of the flat Bengali plain, a glaring expanse of dry, yellow earth under a cloudless sky of unyielding fierceness. For hours he and his son would sing the old hymns of their sect, or of their own composition, songs to which Tagore, the great Bengali poet, had listened and which had enchanted him, for the Bengalis have a rich heritage of poetry, the Baul tradition not least among its achievements. Although unable to speak Bengali, I was beguiled by the sheer sound of these verses, and above all by the dramatic skill of Nabani Das, the intensity of his face, his infectious, overflowing, luxuriant enthusiasm for everything. By western standards this family is desperately poor, but with their traditions stretching back probably as far as the tenth century, and their implicit faith in the love of Krishna, the Bauls know themselves to be possessed of riches beyond reckoning.

*

Two thousand, five hundred years ago, after many years of penance and pilgrimage, the young monk Gautama journeyed to Sarnath, a deer park close to Banaras, and there preached his first sermon and founded the Buddhist religion. It seems unlikely that he would have chosen for this occasion any place other than one renowned as a centre of religion and learning. The repute of Banaras must stretch back centuries beyond that significant day in about 500 B.C. when the founder of Buddhism attained enlightenment under the Bodhi tree at Gaya. Banaras can therefore be called one of the oldest existing centres of learning in the world. For Hindus it is the Sacred City, most important place of pilgrimage in the land, and its position, therefore, is still one of considerable significance in contemporary India. Besides the constant activity and the ceremonies performed on the ghats and in the thousands of temples, the tradition of Sanskrit learning continues, behind the walls of old houses, in the network of narrow alleyways, monastically hidden from the eyes of the visitor.

The November day on which I arrived in Banaras was one of clear, brilliant light, and though I was tired after a journey of over a thousand miles, I could at once sense a clarity in the air which, during the ensuing months, I came to recognize as a particular quality of Banaras. I walked on that first day along the curving bank of the Ganges for the two-mile extent of the beautiful stone-stepped bathing ghats leading down to the water, past palaces and temples, one of the loveliest sky-lines in the world. The ghats are grey with age, the stone temples with their shining gold pinnacles are like processional elephants, the figures isolated on the stone causeways wander as if in a dream, an effect enhanced by the reflected flicker of the river and the spaciousness of the steep terracing. In the midst of noise there is a calm, even on the most crowded ghats, reminiscent of the Venetian lagoon. The greyness is further enhanced at one point by the drifts of smoke rising from the burning ghats where the Hindus cremate their dead. Banaras is the city of Siva, supreme lord, of whom one frequently sees images representing him as the Great Ascetic, clothed in a leopard skin, the Ganges flowing from his matted locks, his body blue-grey with ash. And Banaras itself, grey, aged, is a kind of visual image of Siva, just as the Himalayan snows seem to be the shining abode of the gods. Siva is the guardian and lord of all ascetics, mendicants and holy men, and it is therefore not surprising that one sees in Banaras many such figures, clad in the orange robe, with long, matted locks, their faces masks of ash, within which gleams the fire of devotion. For whatever may be said against the sadhu or wandering holy man, in Banaras one often sees them represented by individuals of fine, almost sensational nobility.

At Rajghat on the city boundary is an old tree, situated close to what at one time may have been a great temple, judging from the number of sculptures that have been unearthed near by. Every night, for as long as people remember, an evening ceremony has been performed by a sadhu with matted locks and long beard. To the sound of gong and bells he walks round the tree with a small light that casts fantastic shadows, forming a flickering, ghostly dance on the boughs of the ancient tree, at the foot of which are small stone images. The scene has been perpetuated longer than memory, and the music with its harsh, fierce sounding dissonance, as well as the single light in the surrounding darkness, suggests a rite as old as man, when his only shelter was trees or caves, a rite unchanged since the days when the Buddha lived with hermits and an ancient order of forest dwellers. It is not so much the architecture or the art of India that is ancient, for much of it is no older than that of Europe, but rather such ceremonies as these, which have endured far longer, and for the traces of which we must go back to the very origins of man.

In winter the greyness of Banaras is intensified for most of the day by the mist which rises from the Ganges and accentuates the effect of age caused by the old stone houses. In retrospect this forms a striking contrast to the sparkle of green in the land of the Santals. There the tribe for ever abides in an unchanging spring, while it seems that it is always autumn in the sacred city. The heroes of the epics, Rama, Arjuna, in their golden chariots, belong to the Dawn, while three thousand years of civilization have left the indelible contours of a now ancient race even sometimes on the supple frame of Indian youth. At Banaras, however, one still recognizes in the figures of young bathers, set in the grey stillness of the ghats, the fierce flash and leaping gold of youthful gods. Like silhouetted statues on the glistening wet stones at the river's edge, figures prepare to plunge into the sacred waters, for a moment singled out from the flurry of multi-coloured garments of the assembled pilgrims.

On climbing the ghats and entering the crowded Banaras streets, one is assailed by the bewildering variety of the scene, so much so that in the simultaneous assault of the senses it seems that colours have sound, and sounds colour. After the stillness of the river-bank, the maze of streets acquires the effect of hallucination. An impression of these streets is built up of many glimpses into courtyards, from whose walls ferocious demons threaten to devour one; of sweet stalls, on whose dark walls can be seen tinselled prints of Hanuman, the goddess Kali, or

Sita amidst a fierce red fire against a night sky; of shrines piled high with offerings of roses and hibiscus; and figures swathed in orange shawls patterned with sacred texts in the Devanagari script. In the shops are glossy wooden toys banked like a diminutive Durbar, Krishna dancing on the seven-headed serpent, angelic figures with blue wings, parrots, elephants, horses, tigers with fearsome jaws, river barges shaped like peacocks. And down the narrow, winding Biswanath Lane comes a chanting procession of priests carrying offerings to the temple. Above are thickets of pinnacles belonging to inaccessible shrines, their walls painted red, about which there are stories of snakes shut away in secret crypts. Through the crowds wander old men who have come to the sacred city to die, men resembling Father Christmas or King Lear, while one who carried the trident of Siva looked like Neptune. Once I saw what seemed to be a conversation between Leonardo da Vinci and Dante, while Nebuchadnezzar wandered by, quietly reciting some Sanskrit verse. Often one sees a figure well known in Banaras, an old man striding along, his staff fluttering with banners, his head swathed in many garlands of marigolds. Occasionally a procession passes with a bridegroom in brocade and turban, mounted on a horse, his face concealed behind a curtain of jasmine buds; or the dense crowd in the market-place parts to allow four men to pass bearing the dead, swathed in white, on their shoulders. A little boy with a crown and peacock feather gravely dances Krishna on the pavement with a bamboo flute, his face painted the correct blue. In the shops are cones of vermilion powder, and boxes containing enamelled brow-marks in a hundred different patterns for the women. At night the sound of a thousand gongs and bells reverberates from innumerable shrines, and from the windows comes the sound of Kirtan, sacred hymns to Krishna, reminding one that Banaras is the greatest centre of worship for all Hindus. On the banks of the Ganges one can see in the dead of night the silhouette and single light of a boat, and floating from it across the water can be heard the night song of a lone pilgrim.

*

The most remarkable evidence of contemporary Hindu vitality is to be found in the great religious figures of the past hundred years, Ramakrishna, Vivekananda, Sri Aurobindo, and Raman Maharshi, in all of whom the world has shown some considerable interest, including such contemporary thinkers as Mr Aldous Huxley and Professor C. J. Jung. Today a figure of equal stature has her principal ashram in Banaras; her name, Sri Ananda Mayee. Originally from a village near Dacca in East Bengal, she is famous throughout India in a way for which we have no comparison in Europe; for apart from being of pre-eminent saintliness, she has travelled widely, from Cape Comorin even to the foot of Mount Kailasa in Tibet, drawing to her many thousands of followers. What is it that distinguishes her from the many minor figures of religious life in India? She herself is the personification of simplicity, a quality which the west no longer finds it easy to appreciate, but at the same time her great personality and her way of teaching are not confined to sect or denomination. She has a striking beauty, with a face as wise as a Rembrandt portrait, a constantly mobile expression, eyes dark, profound, sometimes like a black fire. But it is her smile that expresses pure serenity, and makes one conscious of being in the presence of a great and active spiritual force. As one watches learned and argumentative pandits asking her questions, one notices the singularly calm authority with which she replies, for there is absolutely no hesitation, however complicated the subject. There is, in her spontaneity, the utter peace of a sage, where intellect has been absorbed into a condition of effortless wisdom. If her teaching proclaims absolute humility and love, it is because this is the supreme challenge to the spirit. But in her own simplicity there is the distinction of greatness, as well as subtlety. As she moves about among her people, particularly when she is surrounded by her pupils chanting hymns—girls who recall the choirs in frescoes of Benozzo Gozzoli—one derives some intimation of what draws so many people to her. Here is a brightness, a source of vitality to fire people of any and every faith, an imperishable quality, perennial in the Indian genius.

*

In the cold weather the waters of the Ganges at Banaras remind one that their source lies far away in the Himalayas; and all along the upper reaches of the great river there are important centres of pilgrimage, stages on the journey to the mountains. As one gradually moves northwards over the plains towards the hills, the character of the country alters considerably. The Punjab was the first part of India to be occupied by the Aryans, and it is here that the great historic battles between warring kingdoms in the Vedic age took place. Here were many historic cities, capitals of ancient India, and here were enacted the struggles of the Pandavas and the Kauravas, the rival parties in the great epic, the *Mahabharata*.

Up through the steep Himalayan foothills wind the pilgrim routes; on the hill-tops white shrines mark the sacred places where, maybe more than a thousand years ago, some great sage, or "rishi", dwelt while he wrote Sanskrit verses which have now become the canonical scriptures of the Hindus. These shrines often have small huts where pilgrims can rest for the night on their long journey to the centres of pilgrimage up in the snows of Badrinath, Kedarnath, Gangotri, and far away, within Tibet, Mount Kailasa itself and Lake Mansarowar, where in the ninth century the great Indian philosopher, Sankara, founded a monastery. In the smaller shrines a single oil-wick lamp flickers round a raw slab of stone, smeared with the vermilion offered by many generations of pious worshippers, while in a small recess, scarcely visible in the ghostly light, resides a diminutive image of the goddess Kali, so thickly encrusted with the patina of age that she seems to be like some withered chimera or demon of the underworld.

As the hills become steeper the pilgrim passes clusters of mauve bignonia, or the coral-red Flame of the Forest jutting from the precipices. Beyond Almora and Rishikesh lie the high foothills covered in dense jungle and richly green forest. Here one is in the natural stronghold of the ancient forest sages who founded temples and monasteries for hermits. The region is charged with the potent memories and traditions of some of the greatest of religious figures in Indian history. I remember one such shrine on the way up to Binsar, where Vivekananda once stayed. Today it is surrounded by jungle, the solemn grey stones covered with lichen and creepers, silent and looming out of the surrounding greens like a very old and grave elephant. The jagged pines lining the paths along the ridges already announce a new region in which, one notices too, the hill people are quite unlike the plainsmen. In the temples the carvings of demons and dragons are more ferocious and grotesque, and one begins to realize why. Here is the point of meeting between great regions, for we are in the extreme north of India, close to Tibet and Nepal, lands of the dragon beyond the mountains. Due to its historical associations with classical India, the region of the Himalayan hills might be called the fortress of its ancient culture.

It is an unforgettable experience to make the arduous journey up into the hills to seek a view of the distant peaks. Beyond Almora the hills rise to eight or ten thousand feet, and in the forests are tall rhododendron trees, their branches covered with lichen, which in April are a blaze of red flowers. In the forest round Binsar, the giant trees are covered with thick, shaggy moss, which has transformed them into alarming monsters that claw at one another as if locked in mortal combat. Some have died, others have fallen, and to wander alone through them is to feel oneself walking across a battlefield strewn with the carcasses of fallen Titans. It is a dark, silent world, where thick foliage encloses one as in a dream, producing sensations reminiscent of those experienced in the depths of the Kailasanath cave temple at Ellura. Through the spaces between the trees, in the half-light of early morning one can see the gorges descending into the mist, while veils of cloud move up towards one in a solid white blanket. Suddenly the veils of mist dissolve, and above, beyond the writhing branches of the trees, appears a gigantic black wall, stretching across the panorama of sky; heaving savagely out of the mists, awesome in their size, and etched with deep jagged spikes, the Himalayan mountains are ranged before one. At first they are terrifying because black, but gradually, as the sky turns to a pale yellow, the white streaks and points of snow are illuminated and the mountains become serene, very still, the throne of the gods. This is what the Hindu calls Sri Himalaya Darshan, the blessing of a vision, and that vision is of something imperishable, eternal, and therefore sacred. The pilgrim has reached that point beyond which lies nothing, nothing that is but the Infinite; for the Himalayas are the supreme peak of attainment, an image of immortality itself.

At this point we reach the last boundary of India, where the blue of the chains of hills, a fabulous opalescent blue, leads towards the frontier, the eye going out to the last barrier along feathery lines of trees that wind like a caravan up the precipices and along the ridges into the mist. In the distance appears the massif of Panchuli surmounted by a perfect pyramid peak; to the west Nanda Devi crouches like a sphinx, her head towards Tibet, while between can be seen the curving, snowy slopes of a mountain pass that vanishes into the jagged grey distance. Floating clouds wind towards India, and reach once more up into the jungle, leaving in the centre of the sky a small hole, like a window surrounded with white, through which the snows can still be faintly glimpsed, until, as swiftly as it first was drawn apart, the mist closes over the mountains, and one is left in front of an impenetrable white curtain covering the sky.

19

PRINCIPAL DYNASTIES AND CULTURAL PHASES
IN INDIAN HISTORY

Indus Valley Culture *c.* 2400–1650 B.C. Chief cities, Mohenjo-daro, Harappa.	Seals, bronze and steatite figures, terra-cotta figurines, Mother Goddess, horned fertility god.
Vedic Period *c.* 2000–900 B.C. Aryan Invasions of Northern India.	Hymns of the Rig Veda. Rise of Hinduism. Sacrificial ritual *c.* 900 B.C. The Mahabharata War.
c. 900–200 B.C.	*c.* 900–500 B.C. Upanishads, Brahmanas. Emergence of Vishnu and Siva.
Kingdom of Magadha (S. Bihar) 650–320 B.C. Capital Pataliputra (Patna).	Gautama, the Buddha, 563–483 B.C. Mahavira, founder of the Jain sect, 550–477 B.C. Panini, Sanskrit grammarian.
Maurya Dynasty, Northern India, 322–185 B.C. Chandragupta 322–298 B.C. Asoka 273–232 B.C.	Monolithic pillars. Yaksha figures. Buddhist stupas.
Invasion of Alexander the Great 327–325 B.C.	
Bactrian Greek Dynasties in the Punjab 200–50 B.C.	
Sunga and Kanya Dynasties 185–28 B.C.	Barhut and Sanchi Buddhist stupas.
Parthian and Saka Dynasties *c.* 60 B.C.–A.D. 48.	
Kushan Dynasty A.D. 48–250. Kanishka, ruler of North-western India, A.D. 120–162. Capital Peshawar.	Romano-Buddhist school of sculpture, second to fifth centuries A.D. Indigenous school of sculpture Mathura, second to fourth centuries A.D. Appearance of the Buddha image.

Andhra Dynasty, Deccan and South, 230 B.C.–A.D. 225. Capital Nasik.	Western cave temples. Amaravati Buddhist stupa. Earliest paintings at Ajanta.
The Imperial Guptas, Northern India, A.D. 320–490. Capital Ayodha. Hun invasions of Northern India. Harsha, King of Kanauj, A.D. 606–647.	Probable invention of the decimal system by an Indian. Sanskrit poetry and drama. Fresco paintings at Ajanta, Ellura, Bagh. Sculpture of the Buddha.
Chalukya Dynasty, Deccan, A.D. 550–757. Capital Badami.	Cave temples of Badami. Carvings at Aihole.
Pallava Kingdom of Kanchi (Conjeeveram) A.D. 300–888.	Sculpture of Mamallapuram. Structural temples at Kanchi, Pattadakal.
Rashtrakuta Dynasty, West and Central Deccan, A.D. 757–973.	Kailasanath temple, Ellura. Decline of Buddhism. Classical school of Vedanta. Sankara A.D. ?788–820. Ramanuja 1017–1137. Cult of *Bhakti* (loving devotion).
Chola Dynasty, South India, A.D. 907–1053.	Structural temples of the south. South Indian bronzes.
Solanki Dynasty of Gujarat A.D. 767–1197.	Jain temples of Mount Abu. Hindu temple of Somnath.
Hoysala and Yadava Dynasties of Mysore A.D. 1111–1318.	Temples of Belur and Halebid.
Pala and Sena Dynasties of Bengal A.D. 750–1200.	Mahayana and Tantrik Buddhist sculpture. Tantrik Hinduism.
Ganga Kingdom of Orissa (Kalinga) A.D. 1076–1586.	Temples at Puri, Konarak, Bhuvaneswar.

Rajput Dynasties of Rajputana and Central India *c.* A.D. 816–*c.* 1800.	Forts and palaces. Rajput painting.
Sultanate of Delhi A.D. 1296–1526. Muslim kingdoms of Bengal, Gujarat, Deccan.	Indo-Islamic architecture — Delhi, Ajmer, Mandu, Bijapur. Jain schools of painting in North-west. Muslim miniatures of Bijapur kingdom.

Empire of Vijayanagar, South India, A.D. 1336–1565.
  Krishnadeva Raya A.D. 1509–1529.
  Battle of Talikota A.D. 1565.
	Sculpture.
	Painting at Lepakshi. Temples of the south with high towers and lavish decoration.
	Rise of the vernacular languages. Portuguese arrive in Goa, sixteenth century.

The Moghul Empire A.D. 1526–1857.
  Babar 1526–1530.
  Humayun 1530–1555.
  Akbar 1556–1605.
  Jahangir 1605–1627.
  Shah Jahan 1628–1666.
  Aurangzeb 1666–1707.
	Moghul building at Delhi, Agra, Fathpur Sikri, Allahabad, Lahore.
	Moghul school of miniature painting.
	Rajput and Pahari schools of painting.
	Guru Nanak 1469–1533, founder of Sikh religion.
	Temples and palaces of Tirumala Nayak, Madura, South India, seventeenth century.

Maratha Kingdom, Western India and Deccan. Sivaji A.D. 1627–1680.	
Sikh Kingdom of the Punjab, A.D. 1790–1849. Ranjit Singh A.D. 1790–1839.	
British Period, seventeenth to twentieth centuries.	
Independent India, August 1947.	

9

11

12

13

15

19

21

22

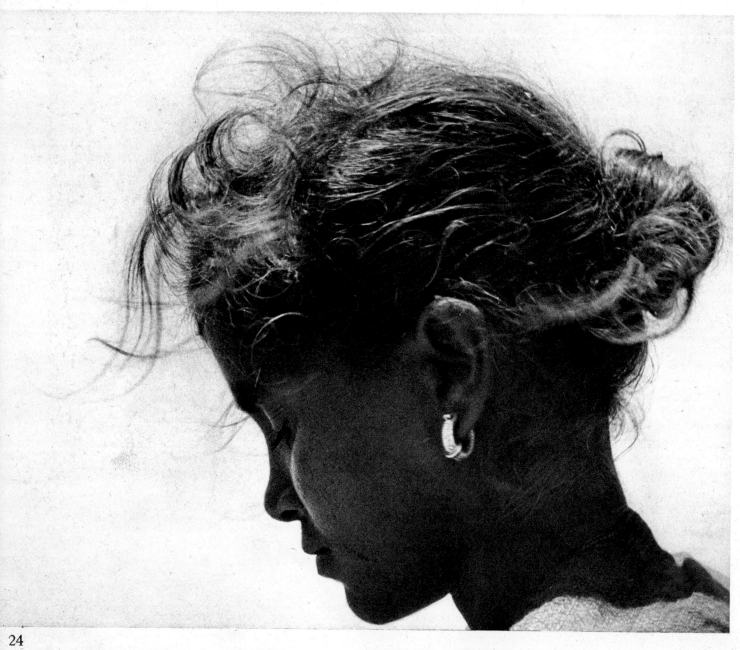

26

27

28

29

31

32

33

34

36

39

40

42

43

48

49

50

52

III Girl seated beside a street shrine in Rajasthan

58

59

63

64

67

70

73

74

78

79

80

86

87

90

91

IV Women on their way to the temple, Jaipur city

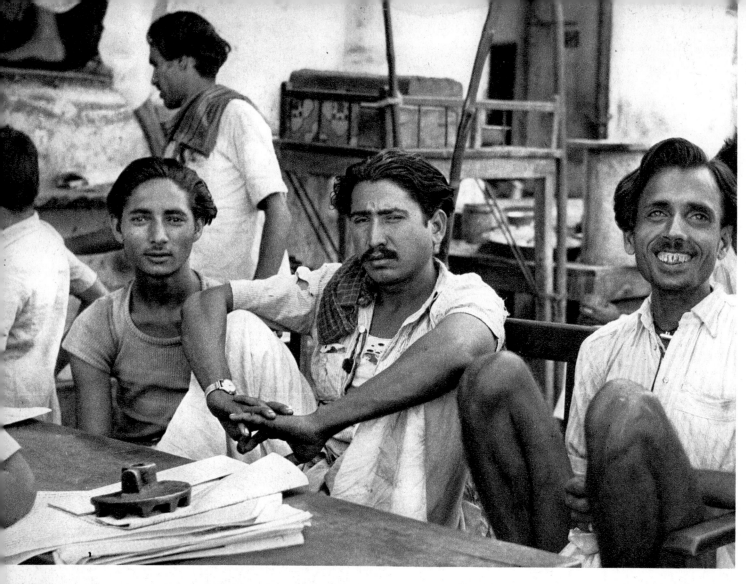

99

100

v Detail from a mural representing the Mahabharata war, Bundi

106

107

108

109

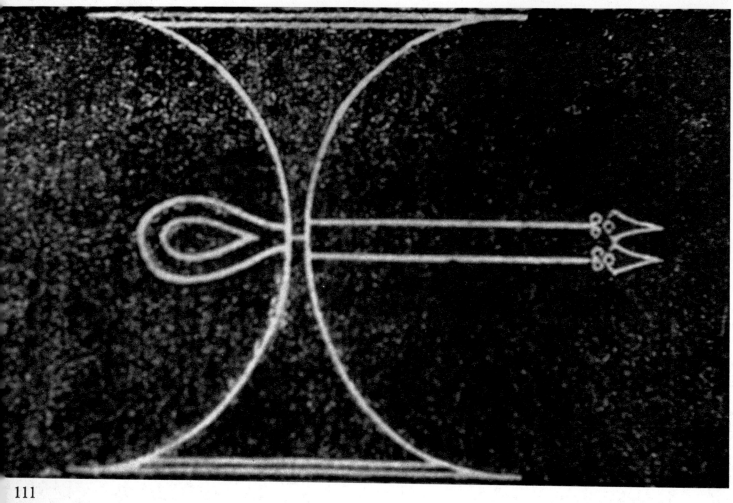

111

112

VI View of the distant Himalayan peaks from Almora

114

115

116

117

118

119

121/122

25

26

127

128

133

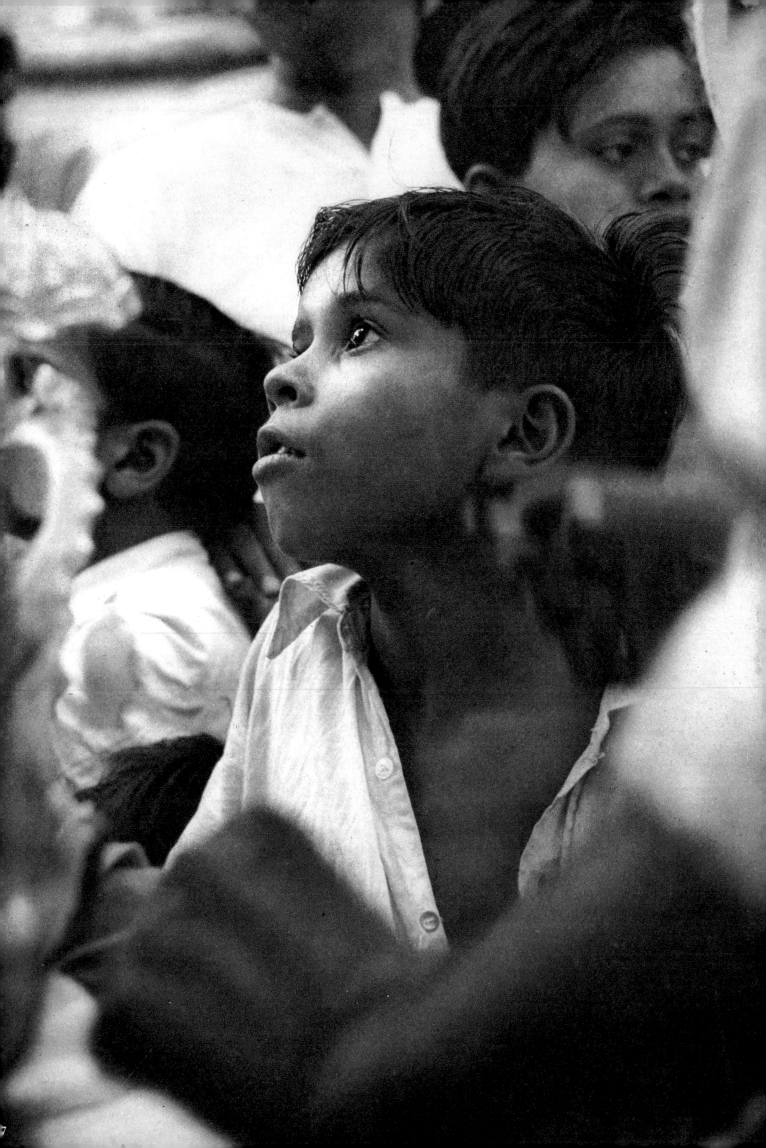

140

144

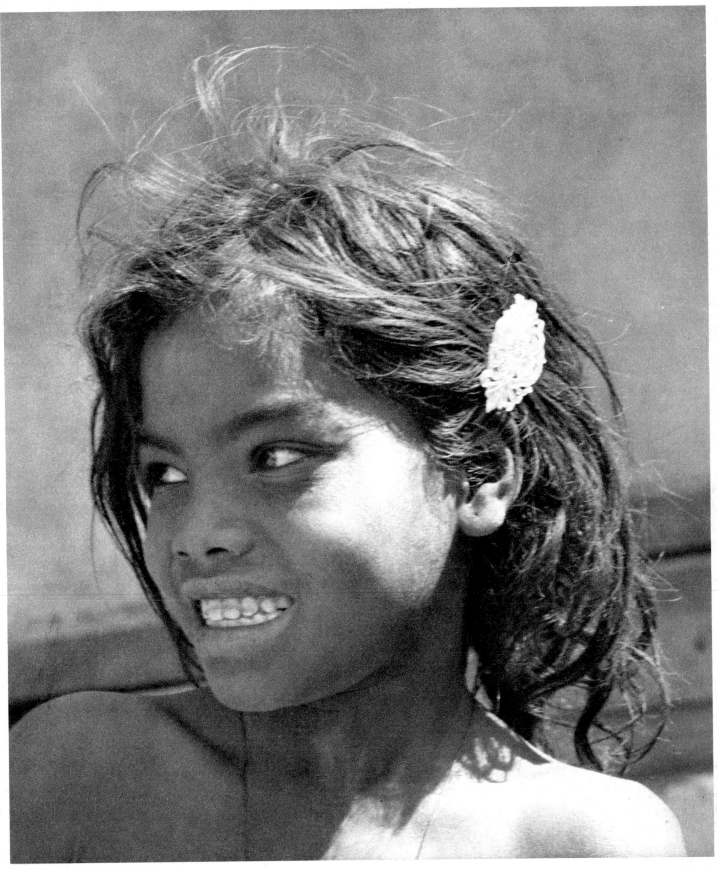

147/148

149

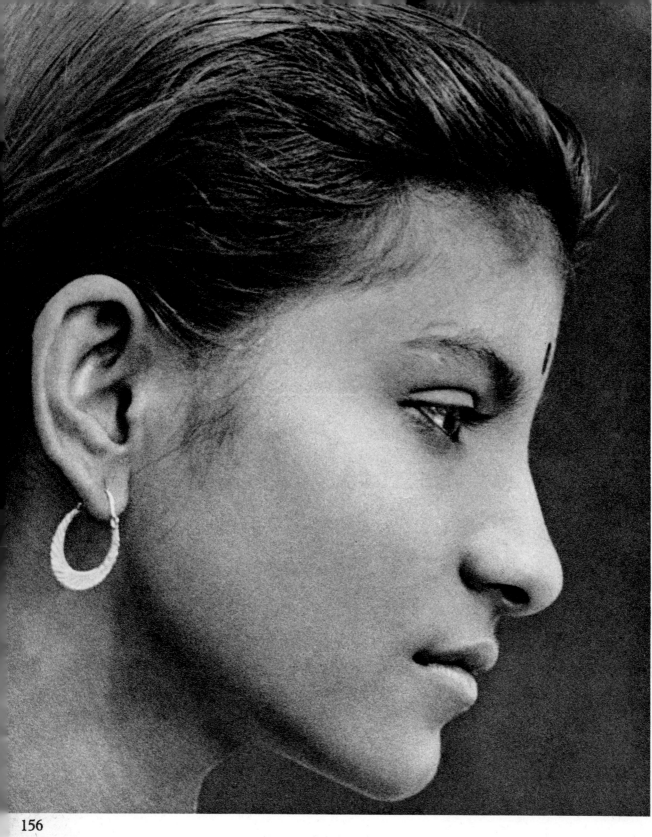

156

167/168

173

181

NOTES ON THE PLATES

Colour Plates

I The eastern quadrant of the Samrat Yantra, a gnomon for recording the hours, constructed in the early eighteenth century by Maharaja Jai Singh of Jaipur. This ruler erected a number of astronomical instruments in marble in a courtyard near the royal palace—all of which were remarkable for the beauty of their design and for their accuracy; he also built other observatories at Delhi, Banaras and Ujjain (the last-named has been destroyed). The instrument here illustrated is part of a huge "equal hour sundial" with two such curved quadrants and, in the centre, a tower seventy feet high, which casts a shadow across them as the sun follows its course. The word "yantra" is here applied to specific astronomical instruments. (See also 113.)

II Durbar of H.H. the late Maharana of Udaipur, at night, during the Dasehra festival. The Maharana, wearing gold brocade, is seated in the centre.

III Girl seated beside a street shrine in Rajasthan. Hanuman, the monkey—a popular deity of the people and embodiment of physical power—is here represented both in a mural and as a silver paper collage, two media frequently used in Rajasthan. Hanuman is one of the principal heroic figures of the great Hindu epic, the *Ramayana*; he assists Rama to defeat the demon Ravana who has abducted Sita, Rama's wife. This ancient epic, which is popular throughout the Hindu community, is often recited by the villagers in the evenings.

IV A group of women on their way to worship in the temple in the early morning, Jaipur city. Morning and evening visits to the temple are customary with Hindus, particularly Hindu women.

V Detail from a large mural of the late eighteenth century representing the great Mahabharata war, Bundi, Rajasthan. The costumes and elephants in this scene, which illustrates the battle of Kurukshetra, must have been based on actual battle techniques of the Rajputs, famous warrior race of north-west India. The school of painting which flourished in eighteenth-century Bundi was an offshoot from the neighbouring state of Udaipur.

VI View of the distant Himalayan peaks from Almora, with the ridge and peak of Trisul on the left and Nanda Devi (26,000 feet) on the right. Along the ridges run the meandering tracks of pilgrims, who annually climb through the foothills to important shrines higher up in the snows.

Monochrome Plates

SOUTH INDIA

1 The village of Badami in the Bijapur district of Bombay was once the capital of the Chalukya dynasty (A.D. 550–773) and the centre of a large and powerful empire in South India. Today, apart from half-buried architectural ruins there remain four cave temples and some early constructed temples on the boulders overlooking the village. Badami was a fortress of the last great Hindu power, the Marathas, who were finally conquered by the British in 1818. The rocks at Badami—which means almond-coloured—are a deep orange.

2 The village tank at Badami, artificially constructed with piles of stepped stones. There are four main centres of community life in Indian villages: the tank, where people come to bathe and wash their clothes, the well, where they draw water, the temple, and the shade under groups of trees. Overlooking the village is the Maratha fortress and in the face of the rock cliff are four important cave temples, three of them Hindu and one Jain, dating from the sixth to seventh centuries.

3 Village street in Badami. The scene is typical of rural India: the terraced steps in front of the houses are used as tables for every conceivable type of activity, from grain-sifting to open-air sleeping in hot weather. The mother in the picture carries her child in the usual way, astride her hip.

4 View, taken from behind a bullock cart at the local market in the Maratha village of Ajanta. Bullock carts are almost the sole means of transport in village India, the designs of the carts varying according to the different climatic conditions of the various regions. On market days the village lanes are jammed with long lines of family carts carrying produce for sale. In villages such as this the bazaar is a weekly affair, equivalent to our Saturday shopping and attracting to it peasants from miles around. A familiar sight on the roads in the evening is the peasant returning home, each purchase tied up in a pouch of his voluminous coat or shawl, carrying on his head a heavy sack of wheat or rice and in his hand a bottle on a string containing the week's supply of kerosene for the family lamp.

5 Girl sifting grain in a village near the famous Ajanta caves, Deccan. On the left are two string-beds on which various grains and lentils have been laid out to dry in the sun.

6 Evening conversation among villagers in the shade of trees and awnings, Deccan. Indians are wonderful storytellers, using their faces and hands with great dramatic effect, and in slack seasons many hours are spent in this fashion. Sometimes long stories and legends are enacted over and over again, night after night, the storyteller himself playing all the different characters. Recitation is still one of the principal evening pastimes in rural areas and although the tradition is no longer as elaborate as it used to be, most villagers are well versed in the ancient epics, the *Mahabharata* and *Ramayana*, as well as a host of other tales of legendary heroes and gods.

7 Maratha women carrying brass water vessels along an avenue of trees, on their way to the village well at Badami. Water-carrying is one of the day's most irksome and strenuous activities, yet it is performed by the women in every village with an innate grace and proud carriage. Even in the bitter cold of a north Indian winter the same routine is carried on, the women still laughing and gossiping among themselves, hiding their faces in the hems of their saris when a stranger approaches. The tradition of shyness and ungrudging service is an age-old ideal for every Indian woman, and although many of their menial tasks require considerable strength, there could hardly be a race of women more essentially and charmingly feminine.

8 The great Serpent King: ceiling carving in a cave at Badami, dating from about the sixth century A.D. It is surrounded by decorative foliage. Snake kings are important in both Hindu and Buddhist mythology as guardians of the underworld and protectors of great treasure, which they sometimes bestow on human favourites. They are usually portrayed as cobras with either five or seven hoods.

9 Flying *gandharvas*: ceiling roundel, dating from about the sixth century, from a Hindu cave at Badami. Surrounded by stylized clouds—to suggest their existence in the sky—the *gandharvas* are mythical angelic figures much beloved by sculptors of this period and region. The sculptures were carved entirely with the small Indian chisel.

10 A village house being resurfaced with mud in the weeks preceding the monsoon. Houses of this type, cool by day and warm at night, are well suited to the Indian climate. They are inexpensive to build, last about ten years and are then rebuilt. Although the streets in India are often neglected and dirty, a house and its courtyard are usually pleasant and well-kept, the brass utensils being cleaned daily with earth or ashes to keep their shine.

11 Scene beside a Muslim mausoleum at Badami. Owing to its proximity to the Muslim city of Bijapur, many people of Badami were converted to Islam and today tombs and mosques appear side by side with Hindu temples. Hindus burn their dead but Muslims bury them.

12 A fine tenth-century temple at Badami. The towers seem to subtly echo the strata of the nearby orange rock cliffs from which the stone was originally quarried.

13 Siva Nataraja dancing the Tandava, a dance symbolizing God as the source and cause of all movement: sculpture at the entrance to a cave-temple of the sixth century at Badami. The village nestles close by, at the foot of the cliff. The eighteen arms are intended to stress Siva's omnipotence.

14 One of a series of amorous couples carved on the capitals of pillars in Badami's finest cave temple, dating from the sixth century. Such groups, carved with a tenderness that is characteristically Indian, are to be found in temples throughout India. The ancient Hindu religion was never entirely divorced from popular fertility cults as practised in the villages and this, more than anything else, probably made the presence of erotic sculpture in temples acceptable. These figures are conspicuous for their serenity, for the Hindus believe that love must finally be considered as a sacrament.

15 Badami woman winding cotton thread on to a loom spindle. Her family are dyers and spinners and help to produce the magnificent fabrics for which India has been famous for two thousand years. The woman is wearing a nose jewel, a popular ornament in South India, and her sari is draped in the Maratha style. The mark on her brow is not what is often erroneously described as a "caste mark" in the West, but a sectarian mark showing that the wearer is a Saivite, or worshipper of Siva.

16 Koli fisherwoman carrying freshly caught fish along the beach from the recently arrived boats at Bassein. This village near Bombay, on the Arabian sea, was once the site of an important Portuguese port and fortress which the Marathas captured in the seventeenth century on the decline of Portuguese power in Asia.

17 Wrestling bout in traditional Maratha style during a *pola*, or harvest festival. The drums are dramatically beaten throughout the contest. The musician on the left is holding a slip of bamboo in his left hand, which acts as a vibrator of the drum skin. Wrestling is popular all over India but particularly among the Marathas, who have a style all their own. The winner receives the token award of a coconut and a clean white "Gandhi" cap. This familiar contemporary symbol of the Congress Party is now used as a sign of national pride rather than for political reasons.

18 A brawl breaks out during a wrestling contest in a village near Ajanta. The occasion is a *pola* (see previous note), in the course of which gaily painted bulls and bullocks are raced through the village, and then fed with special tasty dishes. Usually the atmosphere in an Indian village is one of gentleness but at festival times the crowd tends to become excited, and the policeman, whose baton can be seen on the left, may have to restore order.

19 Muslim drummers in procession on the tenth and final day of Mohurram, a Muslim festival observed by members of the Shia sect mourning the deaths of Hasan and Husain, grandsons of the Prophet. The festival is notable for the procession and final immersion in river or lake of brilliant tinselled models representing the minarets and domes of Husain's mausoleum. The drums, which precede the images (see next photograph) are played all day without stopping by relays of musicians.

20 Processional image of clay and tinsel representing Burak, the animal on which Muhammad ascended to heaven, made for the Mohurram festival at Ajanta. At the end of the festival the head is carefully restored to the family who made and decorated it.

21 Muslim in a trance dance which may continue for some hours during Mohurram. With the help of a colleague he holds a sacred emblem, wrapped in silk and fanned by peacock feathers. He moves about the village in a repetitive rhythmical prancing movement, shouting even above the noise of the drums.

22 A trance dancer swoons in the midst of the crowd.

23 A band of yelling, prancing youths fling themselves into a closely packed group, calling out the name of Husain. After surging on through the crowds for several hours—those who fall being replaced by others —they finally dance round a ceremonial pyre. Then, taking the images on their shoulders, they hurtle down the twisting path of a ravine and plunge them into a lake at the bottom.

24 A young Koli fisher girl from Bassein.

25 A village woman who has been summoned before the visiting Backward Classes Commission of the Central Government, near Ajanta. Mixed feelings of resentment, pride and scepticism are the natural response of people who, however simple their existence, are extremely sensitive to criticism of their own traditions and way of life. The government has inaugurated many rural development schemes, self-help programmes and the like, mainly on lines laid down by Gandhi.

26 The Tin Thal (three storeys) cave, a large Buddhist shrine of about A.D. 700 at Ellura. In the centre, representing only a small part of the enormous and intricate whole, is the preaching Buddha with the seven (only six appear in the photograph) principal disciples arranged in a line on the left. The three-storeyed cave, with its stairways and shrines and its fine pillars carved with geometrical precision, is chiselled out of the rock precipice without any constructional additions. One of the most sublime sculptural monuments in Asia, Ellura is generally silent and empty save for the sound of the wind down the corridors and the agitation of bats disturbed by the lone traveller.

27 Detail of a fifth-century fresco from Cave I, Ajanta. A dancer, surrounded by musicians, unsuccessfully attempts to dissuade Prince Mahajanaka, the Buddha-to-be, from carrying out his resolution to renounce the world and become a wandering monk. The sinuous, softly flowing contour lines, the grace of movement and the languorous charm are all typical of the Ajanta style, which represents the highest peak of ancient Indian paintings; characteristic, too, is the subtle intermixture of earthly delight and an underlying feeling of sadness. These frescoes, remarkable for having been executed on the walls of dark caves, are the most important of the ancient Indian paintings which still survive.

28 The hand of the demon Ravana trying to uproot Mount Kailasa, abode of the Supreme Lord Siva: Das Avatara cave, Ellura, eighth century A.D. The violent aspect of life is often represented in sculpture, as well as in dances and festivals. In this and other similar carvings Ravana is thwarted in his efforts to seize the abode of Siva, for the latter, warned by his trembling consort Parvati, serenely places a foot on the mountain, pressing it down on the head of Ravana, who remains immovable for ten thousand years.

29 A view of the Kailasanath temple at Ellura, an enormous shrine cut out of solid rock, dating from the middle of the eighth century A.D. Mount Kailasa, which the Hindus believe to be the throne of Siva, is a mountain in the western Himalayas, fifty miles across the Tibetan border. Mount Kailasa or Mount Meru, the World Mountain, frequently appears in ancient Indian architecture of the south.

30 Another view of the Kailasanath temple, Ellura. The sculptors cut downwards leaving a mass of rock at the centre, which was then carved into a complete temple with a spacious interior shrine. Corridors and large shrines were cut into the side walls and the surface was adorned with relief figures and scenes from the *Ramayana* and legends of Siva and Vishnu. The temple gives the effect of being supported on the backs of raging demons. The pinnacles gradually become more austere and at the summit, amidst grimacing demons and dragonish beasts, can be seen the serene figure of Siva, enthroned on the peak of Kailasa.

31 Flying *devata* (or divinity) on the wall of the Kailasanath temple, Ellura. The sculptors have peopled the walls of the central rock-hewn temple with celestial figures. The temple was at one time covered with painted plaster, but much of this has now disappeared, revealing the beauty of the sombre, earth-coloured stone.

32 A procession of horsemen from a frieze on the Hazara Rama temple built by the great emperor of Vijayanagar, Krishnadeva Raya (1509-29). These charming figures, scarcely ten inches high, are typical of the lively scenes much beloved by sculptors of all periods in Indian art.

33 Detail from a relief carving at the Kailasanath temple at Ellura, representing the Hindu triad as one body with three heads; Brahma with Vishnu and Siva on either side, symbolizing the three principles of creation, preservation and destruction. The sculpture forms part of a bas-relief depicting Siva riding out in his chariot to destroy the three castles of the Asuras, or demons. To the right is one of the flying Asuras. The plaster has crumbled away revealing the chisel marks on the porous trap-rock.

34 The great temple of Hampi, which has one of the tallest towers in the south, set in the midst of rugged natural fortifications. Though the rest of the city remains ruined and deserted this temple is still the scene of annual pilgrimages. It is situated in an intensely hot and dry region and when the city was built extensive stone irrigation works were constructed, some of which are still used today to bring water to neighbouring fields. The city, whose splendour astonished Portuguese travellers from the nearby colony of Goa, was the centre of the last great South Indian empire of Vijayanagar, founded in about 1336 to consolidate the Hindus of the south against the Muslim kingdoms of the Deccan. The empire flourished for two centuries and included virtually the whole of the extreme south. During this time many of the huge and familiar temple towers of the south were erected. The city of Vijayanagar, which stretched for many miles, was sacked by the combined forces of Bijapur and Golconda at the battle of Talikota in 1565, and left in ruins.

35 The Tungabhadra Dam. Ten miles from ruined Vijayanagar, with its stone canals and waterways, lies this large and important dam, recently completed and here seen nearing completion. Large numbers of unemployed peasants from this arid and impoverished region supplied the main labour force and though the design is unusual, scarcely any machinery was used in the process of construction.

36 Two women at work in a factory.

37 View of the Aarey milk colony recently set up in a large wasteland of jungle and toddy-palms near Bombay city. The colony is renowned for the efficiency of its planning and operation. Buffaloes are kept in special colonies, fed and looked after in return for a small rent paid by the owners, who take a share of the profits. Gardens and restaurants have been provided so that families can enjoy visits to this model dairy farm.

38 Labourers carrying masonry up and down the scaffolding for the Tungabhadra Dam. Slowly, dish by dish of sand, gravel and stone, the huge structure was completed in a manner uniquely Indian.

39 Laboratory work in the Food Research Centre at Mysore. Many government laboratories have been set up to discover how hitherto unexploited resources can be put to productive use. States vary considerably in the scope and success of this work; Mysore, largely through the extraordinary initiative of the late Maharaja, has developed flourishing industries and institutes comparable with their western prototypes except that the methods used are specifically suited to the demands of India.

40 Mothers and their children being taught various crafts at a social welfare centre, at Ashok Vihar, Madras. In recent years, as the education of women along western lines has become more and more common in the larger towns, welfare schemes have sprung up all over the country and play an important part in community life. Hospitals, crèches, maternity welfare clinics are common in the towns and are gradually being introduced to the villages, and every state has projects of a wide variety in every conceivable branch of social work.

41 A toyshop selling clay images of Ganesa, the elephant-headed god, during the Ganesa Chaturthi festival at Aurangabad, Deccan. The toys and images sold at festival time are an important feature of every festival. The images are carried in procession, worshipped and finally drowned in lake, river or sea. Ganesa is worshipped before any important undertaking, business venture or journey.

42 A young South Indian Brahmin, with the characteristically shaved front of the head. In most regions Brahmins are revered as the Hindu priestly caste. They enjoy great privileges and although many exploit their position, they are generally highly educated, subtle-minded people, not always learned in the scriptures but keenly intelligent through having maintained throughout Indian history the traditions of learning and the intricacies of Hindu religious thought.

43 A labourer from Cochin, on the west coast. The most exploited man in the community, the labourer, in his turn, can employ all his wiles to earn the extra anna. There is great vitality in these men while at the same time they can be gentle, hardworking and warm-hearted. The disarming smile springs from a deep sense of robust acceptance and toleration which has been the strength of the Indian labourer for many centuries.

44 Members of the beggar colony, Madras, ordering the photographer to leave. There are many different types of beggar in India, including the religious mendicant. Support of religious mendicants is one of the tenets of Hinduism and these people have their position within society, playing an active part at festivals and in connexion with music and storytelling. The highest and most noble order of mendicants are the *sannyasis*, whose traditions stretch back into the remote past. These wear the ochre robe and can count among their order some of the greatest figures of religious history. (See also 157 and 174.) Although one cannot avoid seeing some distressing sights, caused by genuinely tragic circumstances, a motley crowd of beggars such as this often contains men and women of striking character. The man in the centre of the photograph holds the trident emblem of Siva, Supreme Lord and himself the great Ascetic.

45 The "local tap", in the larger towns a focal point of domestic life. Indians rejoice in water and even on a cold winter day they take their daily bath in the grey dawn under an ice-cold tap. Though their streets are often ill-kept, they themselves are usually most particular about personal cleanliness and for all but the most destitute a garment is not used for two consecutive days without being washed. Rules of cleanliness are no longer observed as strictly as they used to be, but they are still based on the religious conception of purity.

46 The monsoon sweeping over backwaters at Travancore. This region along the south-western coast has a complex system of lakes, canals and rivers that create a network of communication through the palm plantations and rice-fields. The boats are all made to the same design and, like the fishermen's hats and their net "fishing machines", have been much influenced by Chinese traders who came to the Malabar coast centuries ago.

47 A boat, or *wallam*, being punted along a canal in the backwaters of Travancore. The boats are laden with cargo, usually rice, coconut fibre and other produce from the various kinds of palm tree that abound in this region.

48 Uma preparing for her wedding to Siva: from a series of unfinished murals in the Mattancheri palace at Cochin. The murals were painted in the early seventeenth century, only the outline being completed. The story depicted in the series is taken from the *Kumara-sambhava* by the great fifth-century poet and dramatist, Kalidasa.

49 Ceiling fresco in the Papanasesvara temple at Lepakshi, near Hindupore, executed in the early sixteenth century during the rule of the Vijayanagar empire. Costumes, jewellery and coiffures are all executed with remarkable detail. The temple is situated in an arid plain, almost exactly in the centre of South India.

50 Rama drawing his bow to slay the demon Ravana: detail from another series of murals in the Mattancheri palace at Cochin, illustrating scenes from the religious epic, the *Ramayana* and dating from about A.D. 1600. (See also 48.)

51 Jungle scene: palm fronds mingled with broad banana leaves, Calicut, Malabar.

52 Tiger's head: detail from an outside wall painting in Hyderabad, Deccan. These popular murals, based on traditional designs, are still being executed in many parts of the country and are usually renewed after two or three years. They are painted with great speed and vigour, a fact which accounts for the bold and fluent style. (See also 114–120.)

53 Advertisement hoardings in the western manner. The greatest amount of space is taken up by cinema posters with western "sex appeal".

54 Man asleep under graffiti of Hindu gods in the courtyard of a temple (Mombadevi shrine) in the heart of Bombay city. At midday the temple, usually the scene of an active community life, is used as a quiet resting place. These walls remind us that the Indian leads an intensely imaginative life, with religion and the gods never cut off from the pattern of daily routine.

55 Print and picture-framing shop in Hyderabad, Deccan. Almost every family in India, however humble, possesses at least one religious print; these are turned out by the thousand and sold very cheaply. They are often worshipped and it is a common sight to see shopkeepers performing a short ceremony before them in the morning and at night.

56 The hall of pillars, a beautiful example of the late medieval period of sculpture, at the Varadaraja Swami temple at Conjeeveram. Each pillar is a large, intricately carved slab of granite. Conjeeveram, the ancient Kancipuram, is one of the seven sacred cities of the Hindus.

57 A *dhobi* (laundryman) carries away the garments he has washed in a temple tank (Varadaraja Swami) at Conjeeveram. These tanks, with their island shrines, are to be found in almost every South Indian town.

58 Garland vendors in the great temple at Madura. Many of the forecourts of the temple are filled with shops selling every conceivable kind of ware. It is the custom for visitors to the temple to offer the god a garland of flowers, and to receive in return a flower and brow mark from the officiating priest as a *prasad* (blessing). India is probably the only country in the world with a large profession of skilled garland makers. Flowers are scarcely ever arranged in vases and garlands are presented to friends, relatives and honoured guests in the same way that a bunch of flowers is given in western countries.

59 Priests in the temple of Tirukalikunram, bearing the ash marks of Siva on their bodies. The Brahmins who still follow their caste occupation of priests—many practise law or medicine—spend much of their time in the temple, officiating at ceremonies and festivals or delivering discourses on the scriptures and singing religious hymns.

60 *Gopuram*, or tower, Madura temple, *c.* sixteenth century. A bewildering complexity of deities covers the entire surface of these colossal structures which are often over 150 feet high and from a distance give an impression of geometrical simplicity. The Madura temple, like other similar temples in the south, has nine towers.

61 Vermilion painted image of Ganesa, the elephant-headed son of Siva, in a tree shrine at Aurangabad, Deccan. This head is about four feet high and is placed at the foot of an ancient pipal tree.

62 The Kambattadi Mantap (foot of the flagstaff) at the entrance to the Sundareswar shrine, Madura temple; seventeenth century. In contrast with the stern geo-metrical appearance of temple tanks and towers both the interior and exterior of South Indian temples are lavishly ornamented. In the mysterious light the beasts and godlings cluster about the pillars of cavernous halls, sometimes alarming or grotesque, sometimes with great stillness and simplicity.

63 The wall of the temple of Kanya Kumari on the shore of Cape Comorin, the southernmost tip of India. The red and white striped walls are a usual feature of South Indian Saivite temples; here the geometrical severity and the complete solitude combine to create an atmosphere of calm, fitting for the spot where a great country meets the southern ocean.

64 A long corridor within the walls of the temple of Tanjore. South Indian architecture is a mixture of the austere and the florid; the extreme severity of granite and the monotony of endless pavilions are intended to offset the luxuriant excesses of intricately carved shrines.

65 Siva Lingam shrine in a corridor of the temple of Tanjore. To the Hindu the lingam, or phallus, is the symbol of cosmic force. These lingams were put up in honour of the sixty-three Tamil saints.

66 Madras. Man asleep in a shrine beside the road, a figure of Vishnu, god of preservation, at his head. Because of the climate, Indians generally rise early, at about five in the morning, and work in the cool hours, many of them until nine and ten at night.

67 Madras. A young mother and her child, asleep on the pavement at the side of the road during the midday heat. Child marriage is now illegal and women are not permitted to marry until they are sixteen.

68 A boy in a crowded Bombay bazaar pausing before a shop selling pet birds. In spite of the noise and the bustle, business in the bazaar is elaborate and slow.

69 The Rayagopuram, near the temple of Madura, built by Tirumala Nayak (1623–60) in honour of the Raya, or Emperor, of Vijayanagar. It is now taken over by the city tailors.

70 A vendor of patent medicines demonstrating their efficacy by means of a lecture on anatomy from the pavement, Trichinopoly. The costume, earrings and beads are part of the performance.

71 A Brahmin purchasing pencils in a street in front of a temple at Srirangam, an important centre of the Vaishnava sect.

72 Tower and courtyard of Tanjore palace, c. 1550. Tanjore, a great centre of South Indian music and *Bharata Natyam*, the ancient classical dance style, and for centuries the meeting place of scholars and poets, shows little outward sign of these activities except for its palace and temple. This is perhaps only natural since the Brahmin way of life is such that very little of it is seen by the visitor unless he is fortunate enough to gain an introduction into one of the most exclusive societies in the world. The town is also important as the centre of a richly fertile region, the Cauvery delta.

73 The lotus *mudra*—symbolic hand gesture of *Bharata Natyam* (see previous note). The most important aspect of the style is the intricate application of *abhinaya*, the science of gesture, used by the performer in this entirely religious dance to express devotion to his lord. Although *Bharata Natyam* has gone through a period of resuscitation after a long lapse into almost total decline, it is rarely performed today and there are only a few exponents. It usually takes place in temples and to have seen a great exponent of the style is an unforgettable experience.

74 A group of boulders carved into shrines or *rathas* (meaning chariot) at Mamallapuram; seventh century. Mamallapuram was the port of the Pallava Kings. The elephant is the vehicle (*vahana*) of the god Indra, and the *ratha* on the left was actually called and intended to be "elephant-shaped". The harmonious relationship of various sculptural forms is a remarkable feature of this masterpiece of stone carving from which so much later work stems. This group of carved boulders, on the coast to the south of Madras, is popularly known as the "Seven Pagodas".

75 The shore temple at Mamallapuram, dating from about A.D. 700. It includes the Jalasayana temple and a small shrine of Siva. In the distance can be seen the sea and a line of carvings representing the sacred bull, Nandi.

76 Figure of a man gazing at the sun through his fingers, a ritual posture connected with the worship of Surya,

the sun god: detail of a huge seventh-century boulder at Mamallapuram, carved in relief and representing the Descent of the Ganges. The figure is part of a group of worshippers on the bank of the Ganges.

77 Right-hand part of the huge seventh-century relief carving, the Descent of the Ganges, at Mamallapuram. This portion of the boulder (the whole scene measures 84×28 feet) represents the joys of earthly creatures while celestial figures fly about above them. Originally there was a cistern above the boulder and water flowed down the cleft on the left—where there are carvings of serpent gods—into a pool at the base.

NORTH INDIA

78 Udaipur. Procession of royal elephants through the palace gates on the tenth morning of the Dasehra festival. The festival commemorates what in former years was the beginning of the campaigning season. The region of Rajasthan (Rajputana) in which Udaipur is situated was for centuries famous for its warriors. Arid and stony, with many fortified castles perched on rocky escarpments, it is very different from the fertile Ganges valley and the plains of North India. The Rajputs are great lovers of colour, pageantry and all the splendours of a princely state, and their dress, painting, traditional crafts and processions all contribute to make this one of the most highly coloured and romantic regions in India.

79 The seventeenth-century palace of Bundi, standing beside a lake, with temples reflected in the water. Palace architecture in Rajputana shows a fusion of Hindu and Muslim styles. Throughout the eighteenth century, Bundi was the centre of an important school of Rajput painting, and some of the few surviving murals of this school can be found on the walls in part of the palace.

80 An enamelled peacock in lapis lazuli and other stones, on the wall of a courtyard in Udaipur palace. The bird is approximately 2½ feet high and is set in a panel of ornamental foliage. Inlay was a popular form of decoration in Rajput palaces, and this is one of the most lavish examples of the craft. Live peacocks also stroll in the palace gardens.

81 Camels standing in front of the eighteenth-century Hawa Mahal, or Hall of Winds, Jaipur. Before building the city, which is a unique example of town planning, its founder, Jai Singh (1699–1744), consulted many European plans, including those for Versailles. The houses are painted pink with a white design, giving the effect of red sandstone and white marble.

82 Woman carrying water in a brass vessel from the lake into the city of Udaipur. The gateway, showing a fusion of Hindu and Muslim motifs, is typical of Rajasthan, where palace and fortress architecture changed considerably under Muslim influence.

83 Men at their daily bath in the Pichola lake, Udaipur. Behind them is a small shrine with murals and a temple tree under which are arranged small sacred stones and figures. Some of these are so overlaid with the paint and oil of offerings that they have become almost obliterated. Though carved figures under such temple trees are probably not more than a few hundred years old they give one the feeling of immeasurable age, and there is a delightful suggestion of goblins, gnomes and other grotesqueries in their diminutive grinning and leering expressions. Sometimes one sees an exquisite fragment—a hand, a head or a supple torso—before which some daily visitor to the temple humbly drops a marigold each morning.

84 A clown, bearing his staff of office, his face painted, struts beneath a gigantic figure of Ravana, the ten-headed demon king who was slain by Rama. This performance of clowns and strolling players is part of the Dasehra festival, held annually in October in Udaipur and many other northern towns.

85 Women visiting the temple of Jagannath, Udaipur. Temples in North India are usually smaller than those in the south and are characterized by a pointed tower or towers similar to the one shown in our photograph. Even more than in the south, people in the north delight in brightly painted murals of traditional designs, and the tigers and royal guardians on this temple are very popular in Rajputana. The word "Juggernaut" is derived from Jagannath, the deity of this temple. In Puri, Orissa, members of the huge crowds were sometimes run over by the great chariot in which the image of Jagannath was taken in procession through the streets each year; hence the use of "Juggernaut" to express a relentless power.

86 A family sitting out and enjoying the evening in a Jaipur street. A joint family of twenty or thirty living under one roof is quite common in India, although the various sons and their families may lead virtually autonomous lives in their allotted quarters. Families are now relaxing some of these orthodox rules and may be scattered in different towns and villages, but even the westernized, rebellious youth must rejoin the family at the time of his marriage. Love matches are rare, and young men usually marry in the traditionally arranged manner.

87 A crowd of women and children watching staged sword fights during the Ramlila ceremonies of the Dasehra festival, Udaipur. Rama, the warrior god of the *Ramayana* epic, enjoys great popularity among the Rajputs. On the last night of Dasehra incidents from the epic are performed in a big open space and huge figures of Ravana, the demon king, and his minions, vanquished by Rama, are burnt in the presence of the Raja. During the festivities swordsmen and men with flaming torches perform daring duels.

88 A woman of Udaipur ponders on the month's provisions during a visit to the market. Methods of purchase and bargaining are complicated: rice is often in short supply, prices fluctuate considerably, and women with large families have great difficulty in working out ways of buying enough provisions to last out the month. In many parts of India, particularly in the north, people live mostly on wheat and lentils. (Hindus are mainly vegetarian; but among Kshatriyas, the warrior castes, and westernized people meat is eaten, with the exception of beef and veal, for the cow and the bull are sacred to the Hindu. Muslims, Sikhs and Parsees are non-vegetarian.)

89 A Marwari girl (from Marwar, the region around Jodhpur) wearing the distinctive head jewel of her people. On the wall is a representation of Surya, the sun god much beloved in Rajasthan. The Marwaris are brilliant at commerce and their business interests are spread all over India.

90 An old man and his grandson outside the family shop at Udaipur. While the mother and father are busy at work, the grandfather has plenty of time to look after the children, to tell them the old tales, initiate them into the family saga and teach them the legends of the gods and heroes—in fact, to perform the vital task of education and ensuring the continuance of ancient tradition.

91 A family of Punjabi Sikhs on an excursion to the Moghul palaces of Old Delhi. The Sikhs, a sturdy warrior race, supply some of the bravest soldiers in the Indian Army. The Sikh religion emerged during the contact of Hindus and Muslims in the sixteenth century. Guru Nanak, its founder, was a gentle saint, impatient of caste and ritual and concerned to found a simple religion open to all. Later, it was transformed into a fierce military brotherhood. In the late eighteenth century the Sikhs formed an important kingdom in the Punjab. The Sikh is forbidden by his religion to shave or cut his hair.

92 A wealthy Marwari jeweller in his shop at Jaipur. On his brow is a carefully painted sectarian mark, renewed daily before visiting the temple, indicating that he is a Vaishnava, or worshipper of Vishnu. The purchase of jewellery, particularly heavy silver or gold bangles as those seen in the case underneath the scales in our picture, is the traditional Indian way of saving. The Indian goldsmith is particularly skilled at making large ornamental pieces which, though they appear heavy to us, are beaten out of extremely thin gold plate. Jaipur jewellery is renowned for its designs and workmanship.

93 A clerk in Jaipur.

94 A mendicant in Jodhpur, dressed in a beautiful robe and head-dress made up of many hundreds of strips of cloth.

95 A market near Udaipur. Shopping may be a lengthy and complicated process involving much argument and bargaining, but it is one of the main pleasures of the week for the family and often the occasion for brilliant oratory and the colourful display of goods arranged in patterns and cones: piles of red peppers, speckled gourds, shiny packets of scent, bowls of vermilion powder and pungent cases of spices.

96 Café scene, Jaipur. Restaurants are a common meeting-place for Indian bazaar dwellers.

97 Glimpse of a barber's shop, Jaipur.

98 A bandsman dozing in his shop while awaiting a call to play at some wedding or procession. Brass bands are popular in North India and are frequently used at big weddings, where it is quite common for a band to be playing one tune in the courtyard while a loudspeaker is blaring out another from a roof-top.

99 A Rajput baby sitting in a village street. Its eyes are made up with collyrium, which is considered by Indians to enhance the beauty and lustre of the eyes and to prevent ophthalmia.

100 Children drawing on a tin shack in Jaipur. Paper is a luxury, and when the children take time off from their other games to draw, they usually do so on the walls.

101 A boy, blindfolded and barefooted, walks across a tightrope high over the heads of the crowd in Jaipur. Strolling acrobats, jugglers and snake charmers are popular all over India.

102 The house of a family of basket weavers in Udaipur. The finished baskets are generally used by women to cart various products to market and are carried on the head. Crafts are the traditional occupations of many sub-castes, and are handed down from father to son for generations. While Indian hand-made goods are having to compete with machine products, and recent years have seen the disappearance of some beautiful articles of this kind, many others are receiving official support through government emporiums; the government has also allocated generous sums of money for rural projects designed to keep crafts alive and productive.

103 A vendor arranging clay toys on the pavement in Jaipur. The birds and animals are represented with skill and accuracy and, as in most parts of India, they are ornaments as well as toys, popular with both children and adults. Many toys have a religious significance and are sold in large numbers during festivals.

104 A view of Udaipur, the "city of sunrise", beside the Pichola lake and its island palaces, surrounded by a city wall. This is one of the most perfect man-made scenes in India, and calls to mind the fantastic cities seen in the distance of many sixteenth-century European paintings. Udaipur is the old capital of one of the most aristocratic of Hindu princely families.

105 Temple in a grove of sacred trees in the palace gardens, Udaipur. Various trees—pipal, banyan, asoka—are associated with temples and often a grove and a tiny ancient shrine served a wealthy man as a pretext to build a grander shrine.

106 Primitive street shrine in Udaipur, covered with strips of red and silver tinsel, a typical form of decoration in this region where bright colours are much loved. The five strange, bead-eyed deities are surmounted by the sun, moon and a trident (emblem of Siva). At night a small oil wick is lit before the shrine.

107 Street vendors in conversation beneath wall drawings of fish, Old Delhi. With its narrow streets Old Delhi presents an extraordinarily varied picture of Indian life.

108 Man on his way to the fishmarket, Old Delhi, carrying a dead catfish on his head.

109 Siesta time in a back street of Jaipur. The doors of many houses in Rajputana are flanked by paintings of tigers or elephants.

110 A buffalo ambles home in the evening past a house decorated for a wedding with auspicious paintings: Surya, the sun god—crest of the city and the royal family of Udaipur—a peacock, parrot, goose, sacred bulls and "vases of plenty".

111 A yantra of esoteric meaning, from a rare Bengali Tantrik text. A yantra is a diagram or symbol of a deity—usually a complex, wheel-like pattern or mandala—and its various lines may stand for certain attributes known only to initiates. The worshipper, while concentrating upon the yantra, must repeat certain prayers in which he has been initiated, the final goal being to achieve a state of perfect concentration during which the diagram becomes for the adept a vision of the deity itself.

112 Painting on the wall of the Howrah suspension bridge, Calcutta, executed by beggars. Two vagabond artists, one a Bengali, the other from South India, who for a while set up home by the bridge, covered the whole of the wall with these strange paintings.

113 The Jai Prakash Yantra in Jai Singh's observatory, Jaipur, built 1734. It is known as "the crest of all instruments". The two sunken hemispheres, marked with altitude and azimuth circles, the tropics and intermediate circles, are for reading the position of the sun. (See also Colour Plate 1.)

114–20 Seven murals from North India. Murals are still very popular all over India, but especially so in the north. They are often executed on the occasion of a family wedding. Patterns and designs are usually traditional, the most popular subjects being mythical and demonic creatures painted in brilliant colours and bold black outlines. Representations of Sahibs in the costume of the 1900's are also common, and among the newer designs are trains, aeroplanes and automobiles.

114 Mythical beast; Agra district.

115 A bride in her ceremonial attire; village in the Agra district.

116 Tiger's head, Udaipur.

117 Representation of the goddess Kali in appliqué on a banner used at weddings, Himalayan hills.

118 Elephant procession and railway train, Bundi, Rajasthan.

119 Royal elephant on the wall of a house with boy looking out of an open window beneath.

120 Hanuman encounters the mountain Mainak in the form of a demon: representation of the popular legend in which Mainak obstructs Hanuman's flight to Lanka, the island stronghold of the demon Ravana. Hanuman therefore flies through Mainak's jaws and kills her or, according to some representations, emerges from her ear after slaying her.

121 Udaipur. A potter at his wheel, turning earthenware water pots. Stacked on the right are the patterns for different decorations.

122 A wheelwright. Many of the agricultural implements in India are of wood and scarcely differ from those made two thousand years ago.

123 A cobbler on the veranda of his house, at work on a pair of shoes: village near Agra. On his left is his pipe, behind him a mural, painted by his family, representing a scene from the *Ramayana*.

124 Village scene in Uttar Pradesh, showing the use of moulded mud which is worked into beautiful shapes on the porches of houses. The same moulding is also used inside for inset ovens and storage niches, frequently resurfaced and kept very clean. Inside the houses it is pleasantly cool. Furniture, even in wealthy families, is kept to a bare minimum, being considered an encumbrance ill suited to the climate, and many people sleep on the floor. On either side of the steps in the photograph are troughs for feeding the family cattle.

125 Village school near Banaras. Classes are often held out of doors; the boys all have a small slate on which to write.

126 Refugee families from west Punjab, now part of Pakistan, preparing a meal near the Great Mosque, Old Delhi. As a result of Partition there are about ten million refugees, of whom many have now been housed under new government schemes.

127 The tomb of I'timad-ud-Daula, Agra. Built of white marble and inlaid with multi-coloured marbles in delicate patterns, this is one of the masterpieces of Moghul architecture. It was built by the Empress Nur Jahan for her father, Mirza Ghiyas Beg, a Persian and grandfather of Mumtaz, in whose honour the famous Taj Mahal was erected.

128 General view of the tomb.

129 The colonnades of the Diwan-i-Am, Shah Jahan's hall of audience in the fort at Agra. The emperor would appear on the balcony, where this picture was taken, before the throng of his nobles in the court below. The place is now deserted except for the visitors who come to admire the splendours of Moghul architecture, and some stonemasons at work.

130 Agra. A family looking through the arches of Shah Jahan's palace at the Taj Mahal. In his old age Shah Jahan, who had built the famous mausoleum for his beautiful wife Mumtaz-i-Mahal ("Elect of the Palace") in A.D. 1630, was imprisoned in this palace by his son Aurangzeb, who had seized the throne. From this veranda the dying emperor would look across the river Jamna at the extravagant masterpiece, whose construction had taken twenty years.

131 South Indian Hindu girl visiting the marble courtyard of the Pearl Mosque at Delhi.

132 Muslim woman wearing the traditional *burka*, an all-enveloping robe of purdah. Purdah, which was introduced into India by the Muslims, differs from ancient Indian customs. The Hindu prefers a natural purdah of modesty and shyness in women and does not consider it seemly for girls to have any contact with men except within the seclusion of the home. An illustration of this ideal may be found in the *Ramayana*: Lakshman, brother of Rama, has perforce to share the forest home of Rama and Sita for ten years, but during the whole of that time he never raises his eyes above the level of Sita's feet when in her presence.

133 A shop selling instruments for musical bands in Old Delhi. The same shop also supplies bands for various functions and ceremonies. The posters of Indian films on the walls are popular as decorations in bazaars.

134-9 Diwali, the festival of lights, is a religious holiday celebrated throughout the country. It is usually held in November, depending on the Hindu calendar, and is equivalent in importance to our Christmas. It also marks the end of the Hindu financial year.

135 A boy selling paper lanterns in Old Delhi before Diwali.

136-7 Children gazing at the toys arranged in dazzling rows along the avenue of toy-sellers' stalls in Old Delhi during Diwali. It is the custom to exchange presents on the night of the festival and to send Diwali greeting cards.

138 A sweetshop piled high with sweetmeats arranged in spires and palaces for the Diwali festival. These delicious sweets, which resemble rich fudge, are made of sugared honey and milk.

139 Families visiting Rashtrapati Bhavan (formerly Vice-Regal Lodge), the residence of the President in New Delhi, on the night of the Diwali festival. They have come to look at the thousands of tiny oil-wick lamps that line the grand flight of steps. Faintly visible under the colonnade is the floodlit Rampurva bull, one of the magnificent carved pillar capitals erected by the Emperor Asoka (third century B.C.).

140 A wandering minstrel, Nabani Das, of the Baul sect: Suri, Bhirbum district of Bengal. This remarkable old man, considered one of the finest of Baul musicians, was much beloved by the great poet, Rabindranath Tagore, who was himself influenced by the Baul tradition. The Bauls are usually Vaishnavas, or worshippers of Vishnu, especially in his manifestation as the beautiful god Krishna. Their sect, perhaps the most picturesque and least conventional of all the sects of mendicant musicians, has a tradition that goes back for hundreds of years, possibly as far as the tenth century. People like Nabani Das are marked by great religious fervour and a robust vitality; at the same time they are humble and full of humour and unexpected whims. A term of honour among Bauls is "His Madness". It is interesting to note that there are Muslim Bauls too. The sect is confined to Bengal and is principally centred in the Bhirbum district.

141 Nabani Das (see previous note) singing a devotional hymn and accompanying himself on an ancient one-stringed instrument. The instrument of which he is master is the *gubgubi*, a drum with two guts that are plucked; this, simple as it is, is capable in his hands of an astonishing range of tones and great rhythmical subtlety.

142 Street scene with water carrier in Uttar Pradesh. Hanuman, who appears in the mural on the shrine, is one of the favourite deities of the region.

143 Santal women, members of the largest aboriginal tribe of eastern India, dancing to celebrate spring. Village dancing, which is extremely popular all over India, varies greatly according to the different regions. It usually takes place in the evening—sometimes lasting all night—and at festivals and weddings. These Santal women belong to one of the most artistic and developed of the aboriginal tribes.

144 Santal drummers, using two kinds of drum, move in circular patterns in front of the women during the spring festival. Drums in India appear in many different varieties, and the village musician is often a highly skilled performer. The dancers sing as they move forward through the village in short rhythmical steps.

145 A Santal girl.

146 A Santal girl. Indian tribal children are noted for their vitality and spontaneous gaiety.

147 Stone elephants at the entrance to the village square, Hetampur, Bhirbum district of Bengal. The village was once the residence of a minor Raja, and his palace, now empty and silent, lies near by. Villages such as this would often erect splendid temples and statues under their royal patrons; today, with the power of the Raja gone, they feel strangely deserted.

148 Pilgrims seated on the ruined forecourt of a Hanuman shrine, Banaras, damaged in a landslide during the heavy flood season. Banaras, the sacred city of the Hindus, is on the Ganges river, Uttar Pradesh.

149 The Ganges at Banaras, with bamboo platforms and stone steps, used for bathing. High above rises the minaret of Aurangzeb's mosque, incongruously the principal landmark of the city. Aurangzeb was responsible for the destruction of all the great ancient temples at Banaras although the city is still full of temples, many of them extremely beautiful. In the flood season the Ganges, tranquil in this photograph, can become a mighty destroyer, tearing away palace and temple from the river bank. In the heavy flood of 1948 much damage was done; one of the minarets of the mosque collapsed completely and the other now leans very slightly towards the river (not perceptible from this viewpoint).

150 Child playing with wooden Banaras toys.

151 Banaras silk weaver at his handloom, at work on brocade silks for which the city is internationally famous. Nowadays the handloom weaver, even in Banaras, has a hard time competing with the textile mills.

152–3 Sri Ananda Mayee, great religious figure in contemporary Hindu life. The photograph on the right shows her surrounded by the inmates of her Ashram at Banaras during the singing of religious hymns on the terrace high above the Ganges. The occasion is a lunar eclipse.

154 A huge crowd of pilgrims thronging the Banaras ghats during the lunar eclipse. On this particular occasion over half a million people were assembled, performing their ablutions and recitations of the Scriptures with a scarcely audible murmur during the forty-minute duration of the eclipse.

155 Another scene during the lunar eclipse festival: on the Ganges, at the foot of a splendid eighteenth-century palace.

156 A young Bengali girl, one of the large community of Bengalis permanently resident in Banaras. Bengalis are among the most cultured people in India, having behind them a great history and tradition as well as considerable attainment in public life.

157 A *sannyasi* (see also 44 and 174) in the Sri Ananda Mayee Ashram at Banaras. This man was once a distinguished high-court judge in Calcutta.

158 Women on their way to the Ganges to bathe at dawn on a festival of the full moon, Banaras. The Hindu calendar is based on the lunar monthly calendar, and all festivals are determined by it. The sixteen days of the waning moon are considered the most favourable for meditation.

159 Women passing beggars in the early morning on a visit to the Saivite (Siva) Visvanath temple, Banaras. Banaras, the ancient Kashi, is sacred to Siva; and Ganga, the river goddess, is described as pouring down Siva's hair from his Himalayan throne into the valleys of Bharat, or India. The temple is Banaras' principal shrine and one of the most orthodox in India. At present, in spite of opposition to the contrary, non-Hindus and Untouchables (the lowest Hindu castes) are not allowed into the temple as they are not considered to observe the strictest rules of purity.

160 An old woman who daily tends a small shrine to Hanuman, the monkey god.

161 On the burning ghat at Banaras. The Hindus wrap their dead in a white shroud and cremate them on pyres on the banks of rivers. Banaras, sacred city on the holy river Ganges, is considered the most auspicious place to die in India. Consequently many old people come there to end their days.

162 The old mother of a well-to-do family is about to be cremated on a Banaras burning ghat. In India no aspect of reality is hidden from children.

163 A Brahmin girl and her father, with traditional shaved head, sit on a ghat by the Ganges waiting for their recently washed clothes to dry.

164 Shrouded figures pass during the silent minutes of the lunar eclipse, their lips moving as they recite their prayers. Others bathe in the Ganges as the sun rises.

165 Bathers performing their ablutions in the Ganges and making offerings of water to Surya, the sun god. Others are washing their *dhotis* on the stone steps.

166 A barber shaves a pilgrim at the beginning of a festival in Banaras. The bath and the shave (which may be a complete shaving of the head except for a small tuft at the back) are symbolic acts of purification. The devout pilgrim will bathe in the traditional manner at each of five points along the ghats; he will also make a six-day circuit of the city by the pilgrims' way, covering in all a distance of thirty-six miles.

167 A family on the ghat at Banaras next to a colossal painted clay figure of Bhima, one of the five Pandava brothers of the *Mahabharata* epic. During the flood season the figure dissolves and is later remade to the same traditional design.

168 Banaras. Ghat with Bhima (see previous note). At the foot of these great stone flights of steps leading down to the Ganges—many of them erected by Rajas who built palaces along the river bank—are platforms for bathers or priests performing their ceremonies.

169 Women drying their saris after bathing from a ghat.

170 The laundryman's baby lies among the drying clothes on the river bank at Banaras. His eyes are made up with collyrium.

171 Bengali boy.

172 "The Man with Flowers in His Hair", a famous *sadhu* or ascetic of Banaras. The old man, who has never been seen other than thus attired, receives the flowers daily as gifts at the many shrines in the city. People grow fond of eccentric characters and there are many in Banaras.

173 Armatures of clay images which, after immersion in the river Ganges during a festival, have had all traces of clay and ornament washed away and lie abandoned on the river bank. These armatures are often recovered by the image maker and used the following year for the same festival. Immersion of clay images in rivers, lakes and sea is practised throughout India. (See notes on South India.)

174 A *sannyasi* (see also 44 and 157) sitting on the ghat in meditation. His only possessions are his robe, a staff, and a water-pot made of a hollow gourd. By renouncing all his possessions the novitiate is supposed to be no longer attached to the world; with his ochre robe he takes a new name and memory of his former life ceases.

175 A narrow street in the old quarters of Banaras. The rat depicted on the wall is associated with the worship of Ganesa. Each deity has its own animal mount: thus Durga has a tiger, Indra an elephant, and Siva the bull, Nandi.

176 Man preparing to dive into the Ganges. The half-immersed statue represents a priest who stands guard at the foot of the ghat steps.

177 View of the Ganges at Banaras seen through the bamboo poles of the bathing platforms. The fixtures on top of the bamboos are for holding lights during the Diwali festival.

178 Bathing platforms on the ghat at Banaras. After bathing, pilgrims often remain on the ghat in meditation. In the centre is a priest who will perform various ceremonies for the pilgrims.

179 View of the Ganges at Banaras at dawn on a misty winter morning.

180 Terraced fields for grain crops on the steep slopes of the Himalayan foothills, Almora. The terracing is a feature of the region and often extends for many miles up the valleys, covering several thousand feet of the slopes. Almora lies on the route to many of the shrines and places of pilgrimage high up in the snows, and has in recent years become an important centre of religious activity. Famous writers, philosophers and scientists have also lived, or are still living, there.

181 A small shrine to the goddess Patal Devi on the slopes of the Himalayan foothills, near Almora. On a clear day the peak of Badrinath is just visible where the shoulder of the hill comes down on the right in our photograph. The Badrinath shrine, one of the most important places of pilgrimage in India, is a sixteen-day march from Almora and every year, when the snow melts, thousands of pilgrims climb up to the temple, which stands at twelve thousand feet. The shrine of Patal Devi is typical of this region; simple white-washed towers being visible on many hill-tops. Near each shrine there is usually a hut where pilgrims can shelter overnight on their long journeys to Badrinath, Kedarnath, Kailasa in Tibet, or Gangotri, the source of the Ganges.

182 Distant view of the Himalayas beyond Almora, including the peak of Panch Chulhi. For the Hindu the Himalayas are the centre of the world, and Mount Meru (or Mount Kailasa)—sacred abode of the gods—is the final goal of the pilgrim.

ACKNOWLEDGMENTS

It is impossible to mention all those who have in some measure contributed towards the making of this book. Special thanks are, however, due to the following: Dr A. Gosh, Director General of the Department of Archæology, Government of India, for his kind assistance and for the permission of his Department to reproduce plates 26–32, 33, 48 and 50; Abdul Wahid Khan, Special Officer, Ajanta Caves; and the staff of Rajghat School, Banaras. I should also like to express my deep gratitude to Sri Ananda Mayee Sangha for her help and kindness, to Deben Bhattacharya for his valuable advice and criticism and to my many India friends without whose aid this book could never have been completed.